GEORGE F. KENNAN, former counselor to the State Department and Ambassador to the Soviet Union (1952) and Yugoslavia (1961-1963), is presently a professor at Princeton University and at the Institute for Advanced Study, Princeton. His books include *American Diplomacy 1900-1950* (which won the Freedom House Award in 1951); *Realities of American Foreign Policy* (1954); *Russia Leaves the War,* Vol. I of *Soviet-American Relations 1917-1920* (winner of the Bancroft prize, 1956, and the National Book award, the Francis Parkman prize, and the Pulitzer prize in 1957); *Decision to Intervene,* Vol. II (1958); *Russia, The Atom and the West* (1958); *Russia and the West under Lenin and Stalin* (1961); and *On Dealing with the Communist World,* (1964).

GEORGE F. KENNAN

REALITIES

OF

AMERICAN

FOREIGN

POLICY

The Norton Library

W · W · NORTON & COMPANY · INC ·

NEW YORK

CONTENTS

press into this limited and rigid mold reflections arising out of a quarter of a century of diplomatic experience, including the impressions of some recent years in which I had had a small share of the direct responsibility for the conduct of American foreign policy.

The problems to which these lectures were addressed are, for the most part, still with us. Were they to be treated today, China would of course loom larger on the Communist side of the fence; the polemic against the idealization of the United Nations would scarcely be necessary; there might be other minor changes of emphasis. But by and large the lectures stand as the most comprehensive statement I ever made of my outlook on the basic problems of American foreign policy in this postwar period, and as one I consider to be still relevant to the contemporary scene. Some of the views here set forth have found an echo in official American thinking during the intervening years. Others, as for example those concerning the emphasis to be placed on the military element in our policies towards world Communism, as well as those relating to the general place of atomic weapons in the pattern of our military and political strategy, seem to have found only a limited acceptance.

Be that as it may, I am unregenerate and unrepentant. If anyone wants to know what I think about the role of morality in foreign policy, about the problems of containment and liberation, about the uses of the atom in the quest for national security, about the utility of foreign aid as an instrument of policy, or about the relationship of domestic policy to international affairs, these lectures are still as good a place as any to find it out. I even nurture the hope that they may be more intelligible today than at the time they were delivered; for some of the problems and phenomena with which they deal are more widely

Preface to
the Norton Library Edition

NEARLY TWELVE YEARS have now passed since these lectures were delivered. Nothing I have written ever occasioned me more anguish. The problems involved lay on my mind day and night; they woke me from sleep; they accompanied me on all the day's activities. The writing took place almost simultaneously with the delivery. None of the lectures was really finished until the moment came to mount the platform. The delivery took place in that curious relic of Princeton's 1890's known as Alexander Hall. To my combined delight and consternation, the place was packed on each of these occasions to the last of its one thousand sixty uncomfortable seats. The metropolitan press, following the mysterious laws that govern the distribution of its attentions, took cognizance of the lectures, hovered around before each presentation angrily demanding advance copies that did not exist, and added more to my nervousness than anything except, perhaps, the faithful presence of the President of the University on the platform behind me. All this was gratifying but terrifying. Forgetting my age (like anyone just turning fifty), I could find in my own mind no better description of myself, as I stumbled each time to the podium, than that of the daring young man on the flying trapeze.

The anguish of authorship came partly from the unaccustomed notoriety, partly from the technical problem of organizing such far-ranging and diffuse material into four tidy compartments of 50-minute delivery. But most of all it arose from the useful discipline of trying to com-

recognized now than they were then. I am pleased, in any case, that they are again to see the light of day and to meet the test of public scrutiny against the background of 1966 as well as that of 1954.

George F. Kennan

PREFACE

THE LECTURES published in this volume were delivered as the Stafford Little Lecture Series at Princeton University in March 1954. I was at that time enjoying the privileges of membership in The Institute for Advanced Study in Princeton, privileges which made it possible for me to devote myself to this, and other, academic tasks. In presenting these lectures to the public I would like to express my appreciation to The Rockefeller Foundation and The Institute for Advanced Study, whose assistance has made possible this present period of academic retirement.

G.F.K.

Princeton, N. J.
April 22, 1954

I. The Two Planes
of International Reality

THIS SERIES OF LECTURES represents an effort to relate contemporary problems of foreign affairs to certain of the more basic external realities among which our policy has to operate, and also to the internal nature and purposes of our own society. It is my hope that when this exercise is completed, I shall have succeeded in expressing to you something that might be called a personal philosophy of foreign policy.

When one talks of any sort of philosophy it is always hard to know from what point of the compass to approach it. But in the case of foreign policy we are aided by the fact that what we are talking about is a practical exercise—one of the functions of government—and something that has been going on for a long time. Our concepts and outlooks with relation to it represent, whether we are aware of it or not, the accumulation of a long historical experience. I may be misled here by a tendency to idealization of the American past, a sort of nostalgia to which I am afraid our generation is somewhat prone. But it does seem to me that early American statesmen had a better idea than our generation has—a clearer idea, at any rate—of what they were

trying to do in the conduct of governmental affairs generally. And for this reason I sometimes find it useful,
when contemporary problems seem too confusing, to
look back and try to find out when it was, and in what
manner, that thought and reality began to come apart,
as they so obviously seem to have done in so many respects, and how far we must retrace our steps if we are
to put Humpty Dumpty together again.

So I am going to devote this evening to a sketchy
historical introduction. I must ask your indulgence if
this seems to be a somewhat leisurely and detached approach to burning problems I know you would all like
to hear discussed. We will come to the burning ones, in
time. And I can promise you that when we do, they will
still be there waiting for us, and still burning brightly.
None of them is likely to be solved in the interval.

So I suggest that we begin our reflections with a theoretical recognition which, it seems to me, is often lost
sight of in American thought. It is simply this: that the
conduct of foreign relations ought not to be conceived
as a purpose in itself for a political society, and particularly a democratic society, but rather as one of the
means by which some higher and more comprehensive
purpose is pursued. By this I mean that a political society does not live to conduct foreign policy; it would
be more correct to say that it conducts foreign policy in
order to live. Surely, the essential and important thing
in the life of our own state is not what we do with regard
to other nations but what happens right here among us,
on this American territory for which we are responsi-

ble. Our foreign policy, in short, is only a means to an end. And that end must consist in whatever we consider to be the general objects of American society.

What are these objects? Why do we maintain on this North American territory a political society, separate from political societies elsewhere, to which we attach so much affection and loyalty and pride? What purpose do we conceive that we are promoting by doing this: is it merely the routine purpose of assuring the preservation of order among the inhabitants of a given territory? Or is it something more?

I think it is something more. If we look closely at other sovereign entities, in history as in our own time, I think we will see that each of them has had some overall purpose, going beyond just the routine chores of government—some purpose to which the total of its political life was supposed to be dedicated and by which its existence as a separate political entity was supposed to be justified. This purpose may often have been crude and not too clearly formulated. It may in some instances have been more felt than expressed. It may at times have been repressed and temporarily forgotten under the stress of some great external danger. But I suspect it has always been there. Sometimes it has been the glorification of a dynasty and the promotion of its prestige and power. At other times, as in the case of some of the older and smaller European countries today, it has been the cultivation of a national identity and a national way of life. In the case of Nazi Germany it was the development of the military qualities of a peo-

5

ple for their own sake, and the conquest and subjuga-
tion of other nations as a sort of exercise in the military
virtues. Again, in the Soviet Union, it has been nom-
inally the cultivation of a given social theory, and the
facilitating of a supposed natural process by which a
social order based on that theory was to become dominant throughout the world.

You see: there has been no uniformity, no generally
accepted universal pattern. This was only natural. Had
the objects of society not been, in each case, unique
and specific ones, there would have been no rationale
for the maintenance of a separate state at all. Wherever
a unifying purpose *has* become dominant among a
group of states, as in the case of the thirteen colonies,
or where some conqueror has succeeded in making
himself the dominant military and political reality in
a wider area, there political unification has tended to
follow, or the trappings of national sovereignty, if retained at all, have become meaningless, as in the case
of the Soviet satellites.

What, then, is this over-all purpose in the case of our
own country? What would you say we have hoped to
accomplish by maintaining a political society separate
from that of other nations?

If we go back and consult the thinking of the founding fathers, who were after all the people who took responsibility for deciding that there should be such a
country as the United States, we see that government
was thought of by them as a means of protecting the
individual in the exercise of certain rights—life, liberty,

and the pursuit of happiness, as the Declaration of Independence put it—but also, most importantly, the right to hold property and to dispose over it. It was felt that these rights were ones with which men had been endowed by their Creator. It was regarded as natural and just and useful that men should be permitted to enjoy these rights. Many people felt that the English Crown was failing at that time to assure the enjoyment of them to the inhabitants of the North American colonies. And in order that this enjoyment might be fully assured, our forefathers chose to extract themselves, as we all recall, from their previous state of subjection to the Crown of King George III, and to set up on their own as a nation.

You will note that under this theory the state was not conceived as being an end in itself. Nor was it to be the bearer of any concrete social program. So far as I can ascertain, our forefathers believed that such progress and improvement as might conceivably be brought about in the condition of human beings would be most apt to ensue if men were left as free as possible to pursue their own self-interest and happiness, each in his own way. The individual citizen was thought to be capable of a rational understanding of his own self-interest; by pursuing this interest, as he understood it, he would achieve certain things for himself and his family; and the sum total of all these little private achievements, constituting something that has often been called "the greatest good of the greatest number," would plainly serve the best interests of society at large.

It is clear that under this concept the fountains of human betterment were not believed to proceed directly from government. Progress was not considered to be a product of the exercise of political power by man over man. Political power, in fact, was regarded only as the guardian of the natural processes from which the blessings of civilization would flow. The role of government was to be mainly that of the benevolent watchdog.

I say "mainly." It is quite plain that this *laissez faire* concept could never be workable in its pure form. Government, even while acquitting itself of its watchdog function, could not afford to be only an impassive and detached spectator of the results. Inevitably, it had to accept a certain degree of responsibility for what was going on. Government consisted, after all, of people—citizens, like the rest of us—doing important things, exercising important responsibilities. The manner in which they exercised these responsibilities could not fail to affect the way in which the country would develop. In this way it came to be generally recognized at an early date that government did, to be sure, have a certain part to play in the shaping of the national destiny, but that this part was definitely a subordinate one.

With the course of time, this concept assumed the stature of established American doctrine. A half-century ago Woodrow Wilson taught, in the halls of this same institution, that "it should be the end of government *to assist in accomplishing the objects of or-*

ganized society." [1] Note that he did not say that government was to monopolize the accomplishment of these objects. He did not say that government was even to have the leading part in their accomplishment. He was, in fact, quite emphatic in his belief that the state could not "be made a wise foster mother to every member of the family politic." [2] The hope of society still lay, as he saw it, "in an infinite individual variety, in the freest possible play of individual forces." [3]

Admittedly, there have been many changes in our lives, even just since Wilson's time. Circumstances have forced the Federal Government to play a much greater role in the determination of the development of our national life than Wilson envisaged when he wrote those words. In particular, government has come to have an importance in the shaping of financial and economic realities that makes it, whether it so wishes or not, the greatest single arbiter of our economic life—and particularly of what we might call the metabolism of our national economy.

But I would submit—and this is a vital question from the standpoint of foreign policy—that the basic condition of our society, a condition in which certain elementary processes are permitted to work themselves out and the objects of government remain primarily protective and subsidiary, has not been changed. Great

[1] Woodrow Wilson, *The State: Elements of Historical and Practical Politics,* p. 633; D. C. Heath and Co., Boston, New York, Chicago, 1898.

[2] *Ibid.,* p. 630.

[3] *Ibid.,* p. 633.

and important areas in our lives still remain largely removed from government influence and subject overwhelmingly to the laws of free, private competition. I am referring here above all to the great processes of technological change by which our lives are so importantly affected. Over the creation of new technology and particularly over the manner of its introduction into our lives, our government exercises little effective control. Such things as the automobile, the telephone, radio, and television were not planned or deliberately selected for their social implications. Yet from these developments there flow some of the most important forces shaping the nature of our society today and in the future, forces that determine how we should live, what our community relationships should be, what should be the relation between our personal lives and our work, and finally even the educational influences to which we and our children are to be subjected. With respect to all these forces, the law of *laissez faire* is still acknowledged basically to apply. If someone were to come along tomorrow, as perhaps someone will, with another invention no less devastating than these others in its effects on our personal lives, we would submit to it without a murmur. And we would do so because it has been, and continues to be, a basic object of our American society that this sort of development should be permitted to take place.

From such a view of the objects of American society it seems to me that certain logical conclusions flow with respect to foreign policy, and these are, as I see it, very much the conclusions at which the earliest American statesmen themselves arrived. For these early American statesmen the problem of foreign policy amounted simply to this: in the handling of our relations with other nations what could be done to promote the accomplishment of these particular objects?

The first and obvious answer was: that one ought to protect the physical intactness of our national life from any external military or political intrusion—in other words, that one ought to look to the national security —for only in the absence of hostile foreign interference could these processes, in the usefulness of which we believed, be given full freedom to operate.

Secondly, one could see to it that insofar as the activities of our citizens in pursuit of their private interests spilled over beyond our borders and into the outside world, the best possible arrangements were made to promote and to protect them. In this way our government soon found, and has retained to this day, a logical and important field of action in trying to see to it that Americans engaged in private activity of every sort abroad got the best help and protection we could give them. This has meant a great many things in terms of foreign affairs. It has meant commercial policy, commercial treaties, protection of American shipping, and a thousand other functions I will not bore you by trying to enumerate. These things still constitute today a large part of the work of our consular service abroad.

It is characteristic that in trying to protect Ameri-

11

cans in their private activities in other countries our government has normally acted on the theory that this sort of activity was *ipso facto* conducive to the best interests of the nation. It has not, as a rule, attempted to examine each specific thing Americans were doing abroad, with a view to judging whether it was desirable from the standpoint of the national interest. This was entirely logical, because you will remember that the pursuit of individual private interest was accepted by the founding fathers as a good in itself, which the government was there to protect, and into the merits of which government had no need to inquire. Yet this is one of the assumptions we shall be obliged to question at a later point in these lectures.

It is important to recognize that these two functions, the assurance of the national security and the promotion of private American activity abroad, were all that really did flow directly and logically from the original objects of American society. If you accepted them, and them alone, as the valid points of departure in the conduct of our foreign affairs, you came up with a policy very modest and restrained. Its sights were leveled on fixed and limited objectives, involving only the protection of the vital processes of our life. There was no room in such a policy for international benevolence, for lofty pretensions, or for the assumption of any attitude either of moral superiority or moral inferiority to any other nation. Since under this concept the development of American society was essentially an experiment—a bet, if you will, on the likelihood that certain processes would bring beneficial results if permitted to work themselves out—there was no room in it for any messianic tendencies, or for any belief that we had ideological answers to everybody else's problems. We were not like the Russians: we did not come along bearing in our hands a patent medicine of social reform which we were prepared to recommend to all comers as the cure for every ailment. We simply had certain convictions relating to our own society. We were concerned that we should be permitted to work these convictions out. We were concerned that our foreign environment should be as favorable as possible to that process. We conducted our foreign affairs to this end. That was all.

On the other hand, this concept did not rule out a very alert and vigorous and imaginative attention to the real sources of our national security. Nowhere did it imply that we should not look carefully and coldly at the world beyond our borders, as George Washington obviously did, with a view to detecting possible sources of danger to ourselves and to acting smartly and incisively, if necessary, to forestall their development. There was nothing in it that said we should be ashamed to recognize the realities of power or to deal frankly with them in the interests of the survival and intactness of our national life.

On the contrary, American statesmen in the early part of the nineteenth century dealt very frankly and very confidently with power realities. They assumed, correctly, that the European powers would have no love for us, no great respect for the values of our system, little regard for the importance of our continued existence and prosperity as a separate state. They properly feared European intrigues in the New World. They worked vigorously to restrain the European powers in their territorial ambitions here. They proceeded with little compunction to extend our own sovereignty to the Pacific, as an alternative to the penetration of the western territories by European governments. They encouraged the severance generally of the political bonds between the people of this hemisphere and Europe, and they made our country the guarantor of the permanence of this separation, wherever it occurred. All of this involved power considerations. Yet none of it at the time was considered evil, or Machiavellian, or cynical. It was simply regarded as a response to the obvious and logical requirements of our situation.

Had we been able to keep these simple and basic purposes more clearly in mind, I think there might have been much less confusion among us as we moved into the problems of the twentieth century.

But unfortunately with the advance of the nineteenth century, the consciousness of the power factor in the scheme of our foreign relations seemed to pass gradually out of the American mind. This was perhaps only natural and inevitable. The triumph of the British at the end of the Napoleonic Wars put an end to the long period of unrest in Europe in which the infancy of our country had proceeded. It established for us that shield of British naval supremacy which was so effective that many of us came to forget its very existence. The rounding out of our own territory on this continent effectively brought to an end all question of any further serious territorial encroachment by Europeans in our own immediate neighborhood. Except for the brief interlude of Napoleon III and his venture into Mexico at the time of the Civil War, there was no further major challenge to the validity of the Monroe Doctrine. All these things served to dull the consciousness of power relationships among our people.

And, as this consciousness faded from their minds, Americans seemed to lose their feeling for reality generally about foreign policy. A posture flowing strictly from the objects of our society, as originally conceived, ceased to satisfy them. Here, as in other respects, the romantic spirit seized them. They were, after all, the children of the Victorian age, susceptible in every way to a curious diffuseness and imprecision of outlook. They wanted their architecture gaudy, pretentious, unfunctional, overladen with ornament. And similarly, I am afraid, they wanted their statesmanship impressive, unfunctional, with the emphasis on outward appearance rather than on inner reality. A situation arose in which we Americans were no longer content just to *be* something. We were now concerned to *appear* as something—something lofty, something noble, something of universal significance. And it is characteristic of our national self-centeredness that it was primarily before

ourselves—before the mirror of our own adolescent
self-esteem—not before others, that we were most concerned to appear in this way.

So it was that American statesmen came to devote
themselves increasingly to the cultivation of what I
might call, for the sake of convenience, the American
dream. It was a dream marked by a certain innocence,
if you will. It was innocent of every conscious evil intent. But like all manifestations of innocence, it contained a goodly measure of ignorance (which is always
less appealing). It was highly subjective. We were satisfied, by this time, with our own borders; and we found
it pleasant to picture the outside world as one in which
other peoples were similarly satisfied with theirs, or
ought to be. With everyone thus satisfied, the main
problem of world peace, as it appeared to us, was
plainly the arrangement of a suitable framework of contractual engagements in which this happy *status quo,*
the final fruit of human progress, could be sealed and
perpetuated. If such a framework could be provided,
then, it seemed, the ugly conflicts of international politics would cease to threaten world peace. Because then,
you see, everything would have been foreseen: there
would be a legal or contractual provision for everything. Problems could then be solved not with regard
to the ugly political realities of the moment but strictly
on the basis of general norms of state behavior, laid
down and accepted in advance.

All that was needed was the framework, and this we
Americans were eminently equipped to provide. Did

we not have the unique and indispensable experience? Had not our Constitution played precisely this part in abolishing violence between the several states? Our national genius, our sense of decency, our feeling for compromise and the law, our frankness and honesty —had not these qualities succeeded in producing on this continent a society unparalleled for its lack of strain and violence and for its buoyant, confident outlook on the future of mankind? Of course, there had been this regrettable episode of the Civil War; but that was our own business, and that was over now. The march of progress had been resumed. There was no reason why the outside world, with our assistance, should not similarly compose itself to a life without violence. In this way we saw ourselves moving benevolently, helpfully, among the waiting peoples of the world, our experience now finally recognized as relevant to a wider sphere of humanity, our virtues no longer just the virtues of the American frontier but the virtues of the world at large.

I do not mean to ridicule this outlook or to deny that it contained many elements of real generosity, of courage, and perhaps—over the long term—even of insight. It was not wholly irrelevant to the world in which it was meant to operate, and is not wholly irrelevant to our world today. Wherever nations are fully reconciled to each other's existence and borders and status in the world, and wherever their relations are not seriously clouded by ulterior political involvements, there is room for such a framework of legal obligation,

17

designed to prevent the minor disputes from becoming major ones.

But it was important to bear in mind at all times the natural limitations that surrounded the operation of these principles, and above all not to look to them as substitutes for diplomacy or as magic keys to world peace. Yet this was precisely what large parts of the American public and a number of prominent American statesmen did. And the result was that over the course of several decades American statesmanship was preoccupied, and the attention of the American public diverted, with the cultivation of projects largely utopian in nature and decidedly barren of practical results.

The most elaborate of these projects was the negotiation of an extensive framework of treaties of arbitration and conciliation. Now I would not like to be misunderstood. My point is not that there was no place for arbitration. There was. It was a useful and important device for the settlement of certain types of dispute, under certain specific conditions. But the tendency of many Americans was to glorify the arbitral principle beyond its capabilities, to push it to extremes, to hope for too much from it. The fault, like most of the faults of American statesmanship, was one of emphasis, not of concept or intent. And as a result of this misplaced emphasis the United States Government, during the period from the turn of the century to the 1930's, signed and ratified a total of ninety-seven international agreements dealing with arbitration or conciliation, and negotiated a number of others which, for one reason or another, never took effect. Of the ninety-seven, seven were multilateral ones; the remainder, bilateral. The time, trouble, and correspondence that went into the negotiation of this great body of contractual material was stupendous. Yet so far as I can ascertain, only two of these treaties or conventions were ever invoked in any way. Only two disputes were actually arbitrated on the basis of any of these instruments; and there is no reason to suppose that these disputes would not have been arbitrated anyway, on the basis of special agreements, had the general treaties not existed. The other ninety-five treaties, including incidentally every single one negotiated by Secretaries of State Bryan, Kellogg, and Stimson, appear to have remained wholly barren of any practical result. Nor is there any evidence that this ant-like labor had the faintest effect on the development of the terrible wars and upheavals by which the first half of this century was marked.

A second line of utopian endeavor that preoccupied American statesmanship over long periods of time was the attempt to arrive at multilateral arrangements for disarmament, particularly among the great European powers. Our own most direct involvement was of course in the field of naval armaments, but we also took an active part in the general disarmament discussions that were carried on in Geneva under the auspices of the League of Nations during the decade from 1925 to 1935.

Now here, again, the goal was a worthy one. And if the effort, like that devoted to arbitration, again represented much wasted time and misplaced attention, the fault was certainly by no means exclusively ours. Other powers, notably the French and the British, were even more directly involved.

But the fact is that it had been pointed out by thoughtful people, many years before these discussions began, that armaments were a symptom rather than a cause, primarily the reflection of international differences, and only secondarily the source of them. I know of no sound reason why, even in 1925, anyone should have supposed that there was any likelihood that general disarmament could be brought about by multilateral agreement among a group of European powers whose mutual political differences and suspicions had been by no means resolved. The realities underlying the maintenance of national armaments generally were at that time no more difficult to perceive than they are today. More than once, these realities had been brought to public attention by thoughtful writers.

Yet prodigious efforts were expended on these fruitless discussions at Geneva. The record of the deliberations seems to run to something like 30,000 pages. Some 500 official documents, each the result of laborious deliberation and editing and re-editing, entered merely into the report presented by the Preparatory Commission to the Disarmament Conference itself; and this was only the beginning. And at the very time this mountainous labor was in progress, Weimar Germany was disintegrating miserably into the illness of National-Socialism, and new political realities were being created which were soon to sweep all this labor from the scene of world history, as though it had never existed.

And let us not forget the Kellogg Pact: one of the strangest and most bizarre of the episodes of modern diplomacy. Here was an instance in which competing groups of well-meaning peace enthusiasts in our country succeeded in needling two harried Foreign Ministers, M. Briand and Mr. Kellogg, into an embarrassing involvement from which the latter could see no graceful exit except by pressing all the nations of the world into associating themselves with one of the most meaningless and futile of all international engagements. For months the two unhappy statesmen were obliged to duel publicly with each other to see who could appear most concerned for world peace without sacrificing anything real from the standpoint of national interest. Again, the effort that went into the negotiation was formidable. People were encouraged to place solemn hopes and expectations in the enterprise. Millions took it in dead seriousness. When the Treaty was signed, in the Hall of Clocks at the Quai d'Orsay, it was the greatest international ceremony of the inter-war period. Yet the final solution could not, as might have been foreseen, have been more sterile. When World War II came along, twelve years later, even the memory of the Pact of Paris was lost in the general shuffle.

The evil of these utopian enthusiasms was not only, or even primarily, the wasted time, the misplaced emphasis, the encouragement of false hopes. The evil lay primarily in the fact that these enthusiasms distracted our gaze from the real things that were happening. These preoccupations extended over a period that included the Spanish-American War and the first World War. Great events were in progress at all times. When the first batch of these arbitration treaties was being negotiated, the Russian fleet was steaming slowly around the coasts of Africa and Asia to its doom in Tsushima, in the Russian-Japanese War. When Elihu Root was busy with his quota of them in the years between 1907 and 1909, the Anglo-Russian Entente was being formed, the concert of the powers with relation to the Balkan problem was disintegrating, and tension was growing between England and Germany over the German naval construction program. Bryan applied himself to his arbitration and conciliation treaties on the very eve of the outbreak of the first World War; and the early months of hostilities found our diplomats in Europe still persistently plucking the sleeves of puzzled foreign ministers in the warring countries, trying to persuade them to give attention to these curiously irrelevant documents while the lights were going out all over Europe and the guns were already speaking in the most terrible and tragic of all wars.

I could give further examples of this sort, but I am sure I do not need to. The connection is clear. The cultivation of these utopian schemes, flattering to our own image of ourselves, took place at the expense of our feeling for reality. And when the rude facts of the

22

power conflict did finally intrude themselves directly upon us, in the form of the enemies against whom we were forced to fight in the two World Wars, we found it difficult to perceive the relation between them and the historical logic of our epoch, because we understood the latter so poorly. These enemies appeared to us in the aspect of monsters that had arisen from nowhere, as by some black magic. We deluded ourselves with the belief that if they could be in some way exorcized, like evil spirits, through the process of military defeat, then nothing would remain of them and our world would be restored to us as though they had never existed. It was hard for us to see that these enemies were the reflection of deeper causes which could be only partially alleviated, and might in some cases be actually aggravated, by the miseries of war and the abrupt imbalances of national power implicit in such things as total victory and unconditional surrender.

Only in this way could it have come about, I think, that during World War II so many Americans could have deceived themselves so seriously about the prospects for a peaceful world after the termination of hostilities and have been so little prepared for what actually proved to be the postwar reality. After all, the cultivation of this dream of a conflictless world, from which the evil spirits would have been exorcised and in which we Americans would be able to unfold, at last, our talents for peaceful organization, continued to preoccupy many of us right down through the period of hostilities and particularly during the months surrounding their conclusion. The only difference was that now multilateral organization had taken the place of arbitration or disarmament or what you will as the new password to world peace. By means of multilateral organization, preferably on a universal scale, we were now going to bring to the world a thousand blessings —everything from the I.T.O. Charter and the International Monetary Fund to U.N.E.S.C.O., all designed to bring into fruition in our time the sort of world we had dreamed about, all predicated on the belief that the dark cloud of violence and aggression that had cast its shadow over the world in the years between 1938 and 1945 was the product of the ill will of a few individuals and would disappear when those individuals were banished from the scene.

And it was precisely in the midst of this happy illusion that many Americans became aware for the first time of the nature of what is now called the Russian threat. It is true: the Bolsheviks had been in power for more than two decades before World War II. But this had had no appreciable effect on our thinking about the place of power in international affairs. In the 'twenties the Moscow communists had appeared to polite Anglo-Saxon society chiefly as a group of extremely bad-mannered people—anarchists and extremists, bristling with beards and bombs, misguided, motivated by all the wrong principles, unlikely to remain in power for any length of time, sure to be punished in the end for their insolent recalcitrance. The fact of their survival of the crisis of collectivization and the first Five Year Plan in the early 'thirties, and the simultaneous passage of the western world through the ordeal of the economic depression—these things produced, to be sure, a certain change in the outlook of many Americans. The stability of Soviet power was now no longer seriously questioned. Skepticism yielded in many minds to a certain sneaking envy of the Soviet Government for its greater measure of control over the economic processes that were causing us so much trouble. F.D.R. and others found charitable and comforting explanations for Soviet behavior. At bottom, they concluded, the Soviet leaders were no different from anybody else. If they sometimes behaved badly it was because people had not treated them properly, because the French and British and our own Republicans had snubbed them and offended them in the early years of their power and caused them to be over-sensitive and defensive. A little balm to wounded hearts, a little polite treatment, a little flattery in the form of admission to the counsels of the Allies—this would fix everything.

In all of this, you see, there was still little appreciation of Soviet power as a threat to us in the geopolitical sense. On the contrary, throughout the years of the 'thirties there was a constant hope that the Soviet leaders could be lured into some sort of collaboration not only in the destruction of the evil apparition of Hitlerism but even in the construction of the brave new world for which Americans then hoped. Moscow played ably on these illusions with its policies of the 'thirties:

its entry into the League of Nations, its talk of the indivisibility of peace, its sudden moral indignation over the totalitarian excesses of National-Socialism. To be sure, there was then the shock caused by the initial attitude of Moscow toward the second World War—the Non-Aggression Pact, the partition of Poland, the attack on Finland, the cynical absorption of the Baltic countries. These things were irritating and disturbing to the western liberal mind. But they left no lasting imprint. When Pearl Harbor and its consequences suddenly swept all this aside and made us in effect the allies of Moscow in the struggle against Hitler, and when the great American capacity for enthusiasm and self-hypnosis applied itself to the building up of the image of Stalin's Russia as an earnest, upright partner in the quest for a world we could understand, then in a great many American minds the last doubts were removed. There was no longer any question about it: Russia was no problem from the standpoint of the power relationships of a future world. The only question was one of how we were to arrange that wonderful peacetime collaboration by means of which we two great continental nations, so similar in geography and resources, so similar—as many thought—in history and outlook, would walk hand in hand down the shining vistas of a peaceful international future.

It was against this background that many Americans suddenly became aware, for the first time, of the horrible reality of the postwar world—of the fact that this earnest and upright partner was not there at all, and that in his place there was only another one of these great inexplicable monsters, more formidable this time than all the others, sitting astride the resources of half the world and the prostrate peoples of eastern Europe and China, sitting there and grinning inscrutably at us like some graven image, like something really out of this world: committed to the encompassing of our ruin, inaccessible to our words and reasoning, concerned only for our destruction. And now it suddenly occurred to many people what dangers could reside in the association of the dominant portion of the physical resources of Europe and Asia with a political power hostile to ourselves. There was suddenly brought home to people the truism that a combination of the physical resources and manpower of Russia and China with the technical skills and machine tools of Germany and eastern Europe might spell a military reality more powerful than anything that could be mobilized against it on its own territory from any other place in this world, and that this combination was well on the way to fruition. When people asked themselves how this situation could have come about, they were obliged to recognize that so far as the European area was concerned the events that had produced it were ones to which we Americans, intent on the destruction of Hitler, had given our blessing. And when they asked themselves what could now be done to remedy the situation, they were forced to recognize that any drastic remedy involved the most appalling difficulties and complications.

Two Planes of International Reality

On top of this came the fearful realities of the atomic bomb, the long-distance bomber, and the guided missile. With the development of these weapons, the traditional bastions of our security—our geographic remoteness, our protecting oceans, the vastness of our territory, the strength of our economy—all these things seemed to crumble, one after the other, as in one of these apocalyptic movies where the walls of great cities slowly and ponderously disintegrate before your eyes. There loomed suddenly before people a world of power realities overwhelming, now, in their significance, a world in which the statistics of military force seemed to constitute the *only* terms in which external reality could be understood and expressed, the *only* language of international dealings. With their eyes riveted on Russia—fascinated, like a bird before a snake, with the incredible dilemmas of atomic power—many Americans now became wholly absorbed with power values, to a point where they were impatient of any discussion of international affairs that tried to take account of anything else, inclined to dismiss references to any other problems as frivolous and inconsequential, as a form of fiddling while Rome, the Rome of western civilization, burned before our eyes.

Yet through all of this the other world was still there, too—the more familiar world, the one that did *not* threaten us, did *not* wish our destruction. It had not ceased to exist just because the Russian problem had now become visible. There were still great portions of the globe inhabited by peoples who did not grin at us like some inscrutable, malevolent monster. There were still governments quite reconciled to our continued existence and prosperity. There were still people prepared to explore with us all sorts of ideas as to how the peaceful coexistence of nations could be rendered more fruitful, more stable, more beneficial to everyone. Along with all the nightmares of the postwar years, the needs of this other world continued to press themselves upon us, to compete for our attention, to constitute a demand on the resources of our foreign policy. This was, after all, a world to which our traditional approaches were at least still relevant, whether or not they were sound.

And because this was so, American political thought came to be affected, in the postwar era, by a sort of schizophrenia. It operated on two different planes, quite separate from each other and seemingly having nothing to do with each other. We found ourselves living in two different worlds: one world a sane and rational one, in which we felt comfortable, in which we were surrounded by people to whom we were accustomed and on whose reactions we could at least depend; and the other world a nightmarish one, where we were like a hunted beast, oblivious of everything but survival, straining every nerve and muscle in the effort to remain alive. In one of these worlds the old traditional concepts still applied, and we could still be guided, as it seemed, by the American dream. In the other, there was only the law of the jungle; and we even had to do violence to our own traditional principles—or many of us felt we did—to fit ourselves for the relentless struggle of which it was the theater.

Were these two worlds really wholly separate ones? Was there no way they could be brought into an integral and comprehensible relationship with one another? Was there no way in which unity and harmony could again be introduced into the concepts of American foreign policy?

These were the questions that pressed themselves upon Americans from the dual nature of their world environment as they faced it in the aftermath of World War II. They are the questions to which we shall address ourselves in the remaining lectures of this series.

II. The Non-Soviet World

IN THE FIRST OF THESE LECTURES we were able to observe that the external environment in which we were obliged to act our part as a nation has come to embrace two planes of reality, one composed of a whole series of relationships in which our own security is not immediately threatened and to which many of our older American concepts of foreign policy are still relevant, and the other composed of Soviet power, in all its numerous forms and radiations. I propose this evening to have a closer look at the first of those two planes.

This means that our discussion tonight will be devoted to the non-communist world. This involves, of course, a somewhat artificial distinction. I am sure you will all appreciate that these two planes of reality do not break down into neatly delimited geographic compartments. They are extensively interacting. The problem of dealing with international communism, as we shall see a bit later in these lectures, is largely a problem of what we do in our relations with the non-communist world and not in our relations with the Soviet Union directly. But every attempt to systematize thought about international affairs involves artificial distinctions. They represent an unavoidable exercise. And they are dangerous only when one forgets that they are artificial.

Let us begin by glancing at certain general conditions that mark the world outside of the Soviet orbit.

The first of these that strikes my eye is the utter lack of uniformity in the degree to which the various component parts of the free world have advanced along the path of civilization. This non-communist area embraces the entire spectrum of the development of man from a state of society scarcely distinguished from that of the animals to the most highly technical and complicated civilizations. Measured in terms of the time it has usually taken for people to move from one to the other extreme in these stages of development, we may say that parts of our world are separated by many thousands of years from other parts.

This unevenness of development is, in itself, a tremendous factor working for tension and conflict in international life. It is this Lenin had in mind when he spoke of the "uneven development of capitalism"; and it is interesting to recall that he saw in this circumstance the surest guarantee for those internal divisions and sources of conflict within the capitalist world on which communist hopes have ever since been so extensively founded. Lenin had considerable justification for such a view. It is enough to recall that the free world, after all, embraces within itself the entire traditional colonial world, now in a state of great unrest and partial disintegration.

The second general circumstance to which I would

32

like to point is the population revolution of our time. Surely it is not necessary for me to cite statistics to remind you that we are in a period of almost explosive rise in world population, a development so drastic and dramatic from the long-term historical standpoint that I am sure future historians are going to point to it as one of the great determinant factors of our time. This growth of population, a phenomenon common to almost every part of the world, tends in many instances to exacerbate the disparity between human needs and available resources, if only because the rate of resource development often fails to keep pace with the rate of population growth. This, again, is of course an important source of tension and unrest, with deep political and philosophic implications. And scarcely anywhere is important progress being made at this time in the control of the problem. It is interesting to note, in passing, that even the Soviet Union is apparently not immune to a certain uneasiness on this score. Its leaders have, until quite recently, reacted with great violence to any mention of Malthusianism.

The third general factor to which I wish to point is the technological revolution of our time. Again, there is scarcely a part of the world not affected by this revolution. Many people regard it hopefully as the real answer to the population problem. But I wonder whether things are really that simple.

Americans generally have tended to view technological advance as something bringing only benefits to humanity. Undoubtedly there are many instances in which it has fulfilled this role. But I think we have been extremely slow to note the dangers which the rapid introduction of new technology into human living can and does bring with it.

Man, we must remember, is a creature of habit and tradition. Much of his ability to lead a civilized life has been the product of a long habit-forming process, closely linked to a respect for tradition, for ancient custom and outlook, for the accumulated wisdom of the past. More than most of us realize, especially in this country, man has been psychically dependent on the authority of his ancestors and on the legacy of custom and ritual he has received from them. Consciously or unconsciously, it is to this continuity of experience from generation to generation that he has looked for his sense of security, his inner confidence, his serenity of spirit; and it is from precisely these qualities that the capacity for self-restraint and orderly behavior has largely been derived. Wherever the authority of the past is too suddenly and too drastically undermined—wherever the past ceases to be the great and reliable reference book of human problems—wherever, above all, the experience of the father becomes irrelevant to the trials and searchings of the son—there the foundations of man's inner health and stability begin to crumble, insecurity and panic begin to take over, conduct becomes erratic and aggressive. These, unfortunately, are the marks of an era of rapid technological or social change. A great portion of our globe is today thus affected. And if the price of adjustment to rapid population growth is to cut man's ties to the past and to catapult him violently across centuries of adjustment into some new and unfamiliar technological stratosphere, then I am not sure that the achievement is worth the price.

All of these circumstances seem to me to point to a single conclusion. Whatever else we may expect from our non-communist environment in this coming period, we should not expect that it is always going to be marked by stability and an absence of violence. The problems flowing from the disintegration of a portion of the colonial world would alone suffice to justify this conclusion. And they, as we have seen, are only a small part of the whole.

This means, in turn, it seems to me, that many of our traditional American concepts as to what sort of a world we ought now to be seeking must be recognized at once as irrelevant and ill-conceived.

After all, over the past five or six decades our favored approaches to the problem of world peace have sought to inhibit all violence, to do away with all war. They have been predicated, as we saw in the first of these lectures, on the belief that everyone might be brought to accept the existing *status quo*. But today we are called upon to recognize that colonial unrest is the reflection precisely of a deep-seated and important refusal on the part of millions of people to accept the existing *status quo*. And this is not the only source from which the necessity for changes in status and borders proceeds. Thus the task of international poli-

35

tics is not to inhibit change but to find means to permit change to proceed without repeatedly shaking the peace of the world.

This task will be best approached not through the establishment of rigid legal norms but rather by the traditional devices of political expediency. The sources of international tension are always specific, never general. They are always devoid of exact precedents or exact parallels. They are always in part unpredictable. If the resulting conflicts are to be effectively isolated and composed, they must be handled partly as matters of historical equity but partly, also, with an eye to the given relationships of power. Such conflicts, let us remember, usually touch people at the neuralgic points of their most violent political emotions. Few people are ever going to have an abstract devotion to the principles of international legality capable of competing with the impulses from which wars are apt to arise. This is particularly true of democratic peoples, beholden as they are at times to the most imperious seizures of political emotionalism.

Let us face it: in most international differences elements of right or wrong, comparable to those that prevail in personal relationships, are—if they exist at all, which is a question—simply not discernible to the outsider. Where is the right or the wrong of the Kashmir dispute? I am glad that it is not my task to seek it. And how about the conflict between the Israeli and the Arabs? The very establishment of the State of

Israel, at which we Americans warmly connived, was
—whether right or wrong—essentially an act of violence.

Do you find this shocking? There is hardly a national state in this world community, including our
own, whose ultimate origins did not lie in acts of
violence. The source of every governmental claim to
legitimacy will be found to rest in some situation created originally by the arbitrary exertion of armed
might. There is hardly a constitution that does not
trace its origin to some act which was formally one of
insurrection or of usurpation. Let us recognize that
the creation of higher political forms has normally
been a process of erosion from despotism, and not the
result of the workings of any social compact.

Time and habit, to be sure, are great moderators,
great civilizers, great builders of legitimacy and political respectability. I would be the last to challenge
the authenticity of the credentials they bestow. If this
were really a stable world, if national forms had really
set and mellowed everywhere, if nations were remaining static, or progressing strictly in parallel in such
things as population and economic growth and ability
to contribute to the life of the world, then I think I
would be willing to join with the more eager and hopeful of my fellow countrymen in seeking a legal framework for the perpetuation of the present *status quo,*
in shifting from the political to the legal plane the
criteria for determining what is tolerable and what in-

tolerable in the intercourse of nations. But it is only too plain that this is not a wholly stable world, and cannot now be, and will not be in our time.

This being true, many of the conflicts of international life must be recognized as miserable predicaments in which nations become involved not because any one is right or wrong but because history has not seen fit to bless us all in the same way and at the same time, because the march of civilization is too vast for our comprehension and our manipulations, because the great currents of human life are many and complicated and do not always flow in the same direction. And for this reason it seems to me that the first requirement we ought to place on the approaches to our relations with our friends in the free world is that these approaches should be realistic and flexible ones—ones that take into account the tragic, the incongruous, the unforeseen—ones that leave room for the application of equity and common sense, and allow for the foibles of men generally and political societies in particular.

These reflections, I hasten to add, do not to my mind diminish in any way the importance of traditional international law. No one who has spent many years of his life in practical contact with the workings of international affairs can fail to appreciate the immense and vital value of international law in assuring the smooth functioning of that part of international life that is not concerned with such things as vital interest and military security. In my own case this was brought home in a most vivid manner, for during the second

World War my own personal safety and that of a hundred and twenty-nine other official internees in Germany came to depend very largely, over several months, on such protection as international law could afford. In general, I think, you will find that foreign offices and professional diplomatists are very much attached to international law as an institution, and cling to it as one of the few solid substances in their world of shifting, unstable values.

But it is important to the efficacy of international law itself that we should not overstrain its capabilities by attempting to apply it to those changes in international life that are clearly beyond its scope of relevance. I am thinking here of those elementary upheavals that involve the security of great political systems or reflect the emotional aspirations and fears of entire nations. The mark of a genuine concern for the observation of the legal principle in the affairs of nations is a recognition of the realistic limits beyond which the principle cannot be pressed.

The next characteristic I think we should note in our non-communist environment is a very elementary one. It is so elementary that I think I should apologize for inviting your attention to it were it not for the fact that its implications have been so little thought through by many of our people and are yet so highly relevant to a further series of our favored predilections.

Before I mention the reality, let me mention the predilections. I have in mind here the generous impulses that make us Americans so prone to the idea of the solution of international problems by multilateral organization and international parliamentary procedures. These impulses include a certain national sociability, plus a wholly understandable tendency to attempt to apply to international life the devices of our own democracy, identifying the vote of a government in the counsels of the world community with the vote of an individual in our own electoral process. But they also imply, it seems to me, a certain embarrassment, almost a shame, over our very status as a great nation, a feeling that there is something not quite right about being big and great, and accordingly a certain weakness for newer and smaller nations, and an urge to show ourselves their friend, to be found in their company, and to share their status.

Woodrow Wilson was affected by this feeling. It had much to do with his belief in self-determination, with the breakup of the Austro-Hungarian Empire and the Balkanization of eastern Europe. In our own day it has had, as I say, a great deal to do with our predilection for multilateral diplomacy, our feelings about world organization, and our attitude in the United Nations. It is we Americans, after all, who have tended to press the Assembly of the United Nations into a position of prominence and responsibility in determining major problems of international security. But the Assembly, as we all recognize, is a body numerically dominated by the smaller, newer, and less-developed countries. Any general combination of the Latin American and Asian blocs in the Assembly can out-vote all the rest of us, including all of our Atlantic Pact partners and our Soviet opponents put together, whenever it pleases; and sometimes it has.

To international majorities of this sort we have more than once taken our appeal, both in the United Nations and within the family of American states. More than once we have shown ourselves willing to confide great issues of world politics to their judgment. We have taken for granted their enlightenment and their predisposition to ourselves. We have done so, I suppose, because we assumed that we were dealing here mainly with peoples uncontaminated with the curse of bigness or the sinfulness of maturity, and therefore apt to speak with a purer and more disinterested voice on world problems—peoples yearning only for peace and economic development, peoples that either naturally had confidence in us or could easily be made to have it if we showed sufficient helpfulness and solicitude for them.

In the projection of this line of thought, we have gone to great lengths to cultivate such countries. We have flooded them with attentions, with various forms of aid, with large numbers of officials, to say nothing of propaganda. And we have frequently given the impression that even a purely declamatory resolution, so long as it commanded the adherence of an international majority, was more important to us than action on our own part that might actually have affected the course of events. In this way there has grown up in some American circles a cast of thought which holds the form in

higher esteem than the substance, and views international affairs simply as a long series of voting contests,
in which the decisive thing is not whatever practical
effect the vote might have, but the position in which you
are found to be, the company in which you are discov-
ered, at the moment of the voting. It has often occurred
to me that to these people the progress of international
affairs must assume the aspect of a succession of *ta-
bleaux morts:* the curtain is lifted; the light flashes on;
you are revealed either in a favorable and seemly posture or in an awkward one; the light goes off again, and
that is that.[1]

I wonder whether some of the confusion here does
not come from a lack of comprehension for certain of
the political realities that characterize the national state.
It is important to bear in mind that in international
affairs it *is* governments, not peoples, with whom we
have to deal. Many Americans do not like this. The
American mind entertains a yearning for relations from
people to people, unmarred by the pernicious interference of governments. Unfortunately, such a thing is

[1] On March 24, 1954, the day this lecture was delivered, *The New
York Times* stated editorially:

"It seems certain that the Tenth Inter-American Conference,
now nearing its end in Caracas, will pass a resolution reaffirming
hemispheric faith and hope in human rights. This is a good thing
to do, and those who are cynical about the immediate practical effects of such a declaration can be ignored."

On April 20, referring to another Caracas resolution (against international communist intervention), *The New York Times* stated
editorially:

". . . A resolution was passed, . . . The trouble is, with the
resolution approved and the conference disbanded, the situation in
Guatemala remains exactly the same."

not practicable. There is no way for a people to speak in the counsels of the nations except through that political authority that has control over the inner processes of its life. This is a question of the inevitable association of responsibility with power. To conduct foreign policy means, at bottom, to shape the behavior of a nation wherever that behavior has impacts on its external environment. This is something only a government can do. For that reason, only a government can speak usefully and responsibly in foreign affairs.

But let us recall now a most fundamental fact in the nature of governments. Every government has a dual quality. It is in one sense the spokesman for the nation at large. Yet at the same time it is always the representative of a single dominant political faction, or coalition of factions, within the given body politic, and thus the protagonist of the interests of that political element over and against the interests of other competing political elements in the respective country. The aspirations and pretensions it voices on the international level therefore do not necessarily reflect only the actual desiderata of the totality of the people in question; they may also be the reflection of the internal political competition in which the respective governmental leaders are engaged. That goes for every country in the world, including our own.

This seems to me to mean that when a government speaks in the counsels of the nations, its voice may be an enlightened one or it may not be, and the degree of enlightenment will not necessarily be determined by the quality of the national aspirations of the people it represents. The degree of enlightenment in such a voice will be largely a matter of the outlook of the ruling group itself and of the independence it enjoys, at the given moment, to follow a courageous and constructive course in its foreign policy. Very often the dictates of such a course stand in direct conflict with the requirements of domestic-political competition. We see that frequently in our own country. The more democratic a political system, the more acute this reality is apt to be. It is sometimes easier for a strong and authoritative government to shape its external conduct in an enlightened manner, when the spirit so moves it, than it is for a democratic government locked in the throes of domestic political conflict.

Thus such things as smallness and newness in nations are not necessarily the patents to a wise and moderate international behavior on the part of their governments. They do not preclude such behavior; in fact, they sometimes produce it. But they do not assure it. Because they do not assure it, an expression of the opinion of a majority of such governments in the Assembly of the United Nations, or elsewhere, is not always necessarily a wise expression, nor are we necessarily always the more virtuous and impressive for being associated with it. Indeed, when it is a question of decisions affecting international security problems, requiring the willing cooperation of the major military powers to give them reality, there may be actual danger in deciding things according to the voting of an international majority composed mainly of smaller and weaker countries; for it is quite possible in this way to bring about precisely that separation of the power to take decision from the power to implement decision which it is the function of political organization to avoid.

There is no use blinking the fact that we are a great nation, with nearly one-half of the world's wealth and a sizeable portion of its military power. This is a heavy responsibility. It rests squarely on us. We will not really evade it or spread it extensively by contriving always to appear in the company of an international majority. I am not arguing here against the cultivation of the closest possible solidarity with our allies and associates in the world community. In fact, I attach exceptional importance to it. I am merely urging that we try to preserve at all times a correct relationship between power and responsibility and that we do not attempt to involve in complicated international problems large numbers of countries whose interests may be only remotely affected by them, and who will be powerless to make any appreciable contribution to such remedies as it may be necessary to adopt.

In saying these things I do not wish to imply any disparagement of the United Nations Organization or any lack of appreciation for its significance. I view it as a tremendously important symbol of the equal dignity of all nations and the ultimate community of responsibility that unites men everywhere. I also see it as *one* of the forums in which international business can today be conducted, distinguished from other forums by certain advantages and certain disadvantages, favorable to certain types of international dealings, unfavorable to others.

But even in these real and important capacities, the Organization today is only a beginning. It is only what governments are able and inclined to make of it. There is nothing sillier than the alarmed emotionalism with which a portion of our people have turned against the United Nations as though it were some menacing external force that had tried to do something evil to us. The United Nations is in part ourselves, the reflection of our own behavior. As interdependence and mutual responsibility grow among nations, as we may hope that they will, the United Nations will provide one of the most important channels through which those changes can find practical expression. But it cannot in itself bring about the growth of these tendencies, nor can it at once abolish or restrain the deepest and most dangerous sources of international tension. It is an abuse of the Organization, and not a suitable expression of devotion to it, when people try to saddle it with tasks beyond its strength and beyond what the realities will allow. I have never been able to understand the people who, in the name of an enthusiasm for what they call the strengthening of the United Nations, would encumber it with responsibilities that must obviously break its back. It seems to me that, if anything, we have already gone too far in involving it in the problems of peacemaking in the wake of World War II, problems with which its creators quite obviously never meant it to be burdened.

The second conclusion that flows, for me, from these reflections is that we cannot, when it comes to dealings between governments, assign to moral values the same significance we give them in personal life. I am dealing here with a subject on which I have already had the misfortune to be widely misunderstood and I would like this time to make myself quite plain.

We Americans have evolved certain concepts of a moral and ethical nature which we like to consider as being characteristic of the spirit of our civilization. I have never considered or meant to suggest that we should not be concerned for the observation of these concepts in the methods we select for the promulgation of our foreign policy. Let us, by all means, conduct ourselves at all times in such a way as to satisfy our own ideas of morality. But let us do this as a matter of obligation to ourselves, and not as a matter of obligation to others. Let us do it in order that we may be able to live easily with ourselves. But let us not assume that our moral values, based as they are on the specifics of our national tradition and the various religious outlooks represented in our country, necessarily have validity for people everywhere. In particular, let us not assume that the *purposes* of states, as distinct from the methods, are fit subjects for measurement in moral terms.

I doubt that even for individuals there are any universally applicable standards of morality beyond those obvious rules of prudence, common to most of mankind, that flow from the necessity of the preservation of the family structure and the maintenance of good order in a society. How much more difficult, then, to discover any rules of this sort universally applicable to the complicated business of government.

The process of government, after all, is a practical exercise and not a moral one. It is primarily a sorry chore consisting of the application of restraint by man over man, a chore devolving upon civilized society, most unfortunately, as a result of man's irrational nature, his selfishness, his obstinacy, his tendency to violence. The performance of this regrettable and almost embarrassing chore is not an undertaking in which such things as altruism and sacrifice can find any pure expression.

Moral principles have their place in the heart of the individual and in the shaping of his own conduct, whether as a citizen or as a government official. In this capacity they are essential to the successful functioning of any political society that rests on popular consent. There is no one who believes this more deeply than I do. But when the individual's behavior passes through the machinery of political organization and merges with that of millions of other individuals to find its expression in the actions of a government, then it undergoes a general transmutation, and the same moral concepts are no longer relevant to it. A government is an agent, not a principal; and no more than any other agent may it attempt to be the conscience of its principal. In particular, it may not subject itself to those supreme laws of renunciation and self-sacrifice that represent the culmination of individual moral growth.

Morality, then, as the channel to individual self-fulfillment—yes. Morality as the foundation of civic virtue, and accordingly as a condition precedent to successful democracy—yes. Morality in governmental method, as a matter of conscience and preference on the part of our people—yes. But morality as a general criterion for the determination of the behavior of states and above all as a criterion for measuring and comparing the behavior of different states—no. Here other criteria, sadder, more limited, more practical, must be allowed to prevail.

Of course, this does not preclude efforts on the part of individual citizens or groups to project private altruism and generosity across national frontiers. But even here there are deep pitfalls of which people are often unaware. In fact I sometimes wonder whether in this world community of ours, where sovereignty is the still dominant reality of political life and where peoples are separated one from another by these unsatisfactory but indispensable arrangements we call governments—I sometimes wonder whether in such a world it is possible at all to project across international frontiers the more generous and kindly of the individual impulses without inviting more suspicion and misunderstanding than one removes. And I wonder whether the best that we can do, all of us, is not rather to pour these impulses into the vessel of our own national life, where today they are so desperately needed, in the confidence that they will be best understood and appreciated by other people if they appear in the evidences of what we have done for ourselves, rather than in the evidences of what we have tried to do for others.

In any case, when we return to the relations between governments, I think we are entitled to say that international life would be quieter and more comfortable, that there would be less of misunderstanding, and that it would be easier to clear away such conflicts as do arise, if there were less of sentimentality, less eagerness to be morally impressive, a greater willingness to admit that we Americans, like everyone else, are only people, in whose lives the elements of weakness and virtue are too thoroughly and confusingly intermingled to justify us either in any claim to a special moral distinction or in any sense of shame over the fact that we do exist, that we are a great nation, and that as such we occasionally have needs we are obliged to express to other people and to ask them to respect.

A further characteristic of our non-communist world I would like to mention is again one that has been very widely noted and discussed—even to the point where the words sound hackneyed. It is the growing economic interdependence between this part of our world environment and ourselves. If it were only a matter of recognizing the problem itself, I would hardly bother to mention it this evening. But it is also a matter of recognizing its general implications for our national policies; and this, I think, has not been adequately done in our government as a whole or in our public discussions.

Let us remember that this interdependence does not

work exactly the same way for both parties. For ourselves it is partly a matter of the stability of our own economic life, but more importantly, I think, a matter of our growing dependence on foreign sources of raw material. This can be a very harsh reality, as we will discover if certain of these raw materials sources are ever interfered with. It can be a harsh reality not only for us but for the respective producing countries themselves.

The dependence of the others on us generally takes the form of a heavy reliance on the stability of our foreign economic exchanges, and often not just of our bilateral exchanges with the country in question, but of the sum total of those exchanges with the world at large.

For purposes of this discussion tonight I wish only to point out that these realities introduce into the pattern of our foreign relations a great factor of precariousness to which we should give most careful attention. Danger can arise, as you will readily see, either from external causes such as events elsewhere that threaten the supplies of raw materials vital to the functioning of our national life, or from internal causes—fluctuations of our own economy or our own policy—that would affect the stability of our participation in the world economy. In neither the one case nor the other does it seem to me that we have these possibilities under adequate control today. Between these two areas of cosmic uncertainty there hangs precariously not only the security of our highly complicated and in many ways fragile American economy but also the social and political security of a good portion of the friendly world.

In the first case, that of the foreign raw materials, you will see from the recent Iranian dispute and other instances that we have, as a government, largely conceded the right of any other sovereign government to do anything it wishes with regard to the raw material resources of its own territory, even though this may mean the invalidation of existing foreign contracts and the abrupt disruption of arrangements for the sale and distribution of such materials to other countries. The fact that other countries may have become extensively dependent on these arrangements is not, to judge from the Iranian oil case, considered to be any proper formal grounds for insistence on respect for their interests. Against such things as capriciousness and irresponsibility on the part of the government of the raw-material-exporting countries, or the sudden denial of raw material exports as a means of political extortion, there is apparently no theoretical recourse except such commercial pressure as foreign firms may themselves be able and inclined to exert, and this is by no means always adequate or effective. Wherever the status of absolute sovereignty, traditionally a western concept, is conceded, these extensive powers are acknowledged to exist, and the security of our raw material sources then resides primarily in such sense of responsibility and maturity as the respective governments are able to manifest.

Now restraint and reliability in the conduct of governmental affairs do indeed exist in many countries, but they certainly do not exist in all of them. They are not the monopoly of the larger countries or even of the older ones, but I must say that it seems to me they are more often found in the governments of peoples whose enjoyment of the sovereign status has some historical depth and who have accumulated a certain fund of experience and tradition in the exercise of sovereign independence and the practice of participation in world affairs.

The fact that many of the foreign raw material sources are on the territory of governments that do not yet enjoy these advantages, coupled with the extensive value we attach to national sovereignty, seems to me to mean that in many instances our raw material supply hangs on slender threads, and ones over which we have no power of control or even of redress. And I worry lest some day drastic interruptions of this supply should lead to painful crises and tensions of the sort that have often in the past been connected with the charge of imperialism. I wonder whether it would not be the part of kindness and liberality, in reality, to face up to this problem today by making it plain to other governments that they must not permit our great and in many cases delicate economy to become dependent on them in this way unless they are prepared to acknowledge a clear obligation to guard the durability and reliability of the respective arrangements.

In the case of the danger that can arise for the stability of our foreign economic relationships from fluctuations in our own country, I do not rate this danger so high, as a practical reality, as do some of our more nervous European friends. But it does seem to me that the Executive Branch of our Government should be better armed than it is today to shape the level of our foreign exchange, with respect to trade as well as to aid, in such a way as to assure regularity at all times and to offset fluctuations that might otherwise affect them. This would certainly involve a greater delegation of power in these matters from the Legislative to the Executive branch than we have seen in recent years, and that is precisely what I am arguing for.

I should like to emphasize that what seems to me to be required here is primarily a stability and firmness and reliability in these international economic arrangements, not an endless series of one-sided handouts from one country to others. The ideal, as I see it, is that the terms of exchange should be fair ones, governed basically by the realities of the market, but that they should be stable, secure ones, protected so far as possible from speculative fluctuations as well as from abrupt and erratic whims of governmental policy. They should be terms on which people can plan and depend.

This mention of economic relationships brings me to the last of the observations I would like to make with respect to our policies with regard to the non-communist world. In recent years we have based these policies largely on the effort to cultivate favor and to be liked. Our weapons have been the weapons of the suitor. It has been unthinkable to many of us that they should be anything else. We have come to view our rivalry with the Russians as a contest of popularity, to be judged by the public opinion of other countries. Viewing it in this way, it has seemed to us that the devices of ingratiation were the only ones suitable to our purpose—that this purpose would only be defeated by the opposite devices, the ones of denial and restraint.

With most of this I have no quarrel, but again there are certain limiting factors I think we would do well to bear in mind. First of all, I think we must recognize a sad and curious fact of human nature: namely, that favors granted habitually or unduly prolonged cease with time to be regarded by the recipients as favors at all and come to be regarded by them as rights. This is a sort of mathematical absurdity, to be sure; for it means that the more favor the less appreciation. Not only that: it means that the withdrawal of the favor becomes an injury, to be resented accordingly, even though there may not have been the slightest right to the favor in the first instance.

I would suggest that this imposes certain limitations on what we can expect to accomplish in the cultivation of popularity with other nations through such devices as economic aid and technical assistance. Please do not misunderstand me: I do not think that this is the *only* consideration by which technical assistance programs can be warranted. There are desirable reactions on the part of peoples elsewhere other than ones of gratitude to us which can conceivably be promoted in certain situations by the extension of aid in one form or another. The Marshall Plan seems to me to have been an eminent example of a sound and correct approach to one such situation, and particularly because its major aim was *not* to move other peoples to a feeling of obligation to us but rather to make it possible for them to pursue their own best interests with courage and confidence. But there are many people who seem to think of economic and technical aid only as a device by which we make other people fond of us and grateful to us; and I would only like to remind them that such sentiments, if they appear at all, are not apt to be very enduring ones, and that by permitting other peoples to accustom themselves to various sorts of one-sided assistance from us we will be creating situations that cannot be easily terminated except at the cost of new misunderstanding and resentment.

There is another reality underlying every form of governmental assistance to other countries, which seems to me to have been widely ignored by Americans. It is the fact that it is very difficult, if not impossible, to benefit a people in its entirety by any sort of physical or technological assistance from outside, or at least to cause it to consider itself so benefited. Practically every human society is the scene of sharp struggle between competitive forces, economic and political. Any external intervention into this competitive process, be it only in the forms of goods or services offered free of obligation and from the most generous and altruistic of motives, is bound to affect the terms of competition and thus to injure one side as it benefits another. If aid is important at all, its effect is always going to produce imbalances and to create need for new adjustments. Certain elements within the respective country will benefit from such changes, but there will always be others who will suffer.

Now, of course, it may well be that the over-all effect of such aid will be beneficial to the recipient nation, at least according to our lights. But those who consider themselves to be the losers by the interjection of this new factor into their life are not going to look at it this way; and their bitterness is apt to attach itself to the foreigners from whom this assistance flowed, rather than to their own government which may have wanted and requested it. In 1918 our government made the mistake of believing that it could bring impartial economic assistance to all the people of Siberia by means of our benevolent military intervention into that area; and General Graves, the commander of our forces, was soon obliged to learn the painful lesson that nothing he and his forces did, however concerned they were to remain neutral and impartial and helpful to everyone, could fail to enter into the gears of the fierce political competition prevailing at that time in the Siberian area, and to make enemies as well as friends. Let us recognize that even benevolence, when addressed to a foreign people, represents a form of intervention into their internal affairs, and always receives, at best, a divided reception.

I think, furthermore, that there is a certain dialectic involved in this question of influencing the attitudes and behavior of other peoples: a dialectic which means that the process is never fully effective unless people feel not only that our *favor* is a real possibility, attended by certain visible advantages to themselves, but that our *disfavor* would be, in certain circumstances, also a real possibility and would be attended by certain disadvantages to them. I mention this with reluctance, for there are a large number of countries in the non-communist world that have achieved so high a degree of maturity in their policies generally and whose relations with us are on so firm and sensible a basis that these reflections have little relevance. What I am speaking about here relates primarily only to a certain fringe of the non-communist countries, but that fringe includes countries that stand in particular danger today in the face of Soviet enticements and pressures. Here, I must say, I view with skepticism our chances for exerting any useful influence unless we learn how to create a respect for our possible disfavor at least as great as the respect for our possible favor. The Russians, as everyone knows, have profited greatly, in the political sense, precisely by the degree to which they have contrived to be feared rather than loved. I am not recommending that we imitate them in this respect. But I doubt that any American policy can be successful with regard to the countries that are hovering between the two worlds unless it embraces within itself, for all to see, the harsh as well as the mild elements, with the possibility of their both being applied flexibly and interchangeably and sometimes even simultaneously, as the requirements of the situation may indicate.

To me, this means two things. It means first of all a careful study of the ways, short of unleashing a total war, in which the denial of American favor can be made to bring other people to respect the seriousness of our purposes and the dignity of our position in the world. Jefferson once said that we held in our hands "those peaceable coercions which are in the power of every nation, if undertaken in concert and in time of peace," [2] and indicated that we needed only to develop and use them. I am merely recommending that we bring this thought of Jefferson's up to date. But this also means (and this is going to be the hardest thing of all) a reform of the processes of our own government as a result of which many of those facets of American activity from which people in other countries tend to profit may be brought under a well-coordinated and disciplined control. I have no doubt, for example, that if there were today an adequate coordination of the workings of our governmental machinery and adequate collaboration between our government and important private business interests in this country, the contribution we North Americans could make to the combatting of communism in the New World would be far more important and effective than it is today, so important in fact that there would

[2] Thomas Jefferson to Robert R. Livingston, Minister to France, September 9, 1801. Jefferson manuscripts, Library of Congress.

be less need for international resolutions dealing with this problem—and yet no measures would have to be taken that would partake of the nature of gratuitous pressures or threats. Nothing more would be involved than the denial of benefits to which people have no God-given title and which, in certain well known instances, they have obviously either come to take for granted or ceased to value very highly. But this, as I say, would involve a degree of governmental coordination which we in this country do not today possess; and it is to this weakness that we will have to look if we are to cope successfully with some of the most pressing and dangerous of our international problems.

If I may summarize, then, the direction in which these observations tend, I would say they argue for a somewhat different approach to what we might call the "normal" problems of foreign relations than the one that has become common in our public discussions. It would be an approach not predicated on any hope for the early total abolition of violence from the affairs of nations, but concerned primarily to reduce the scope and dangerousness of such violence where it cannot be avoided. It would be motivated by full respect and real solicitude for the United Nations; but at the same time it would recognize the unique responsibility that rests upon us by virtue of our relative physical strength, and would resist the temptation to try to spread this responsibility too far through the devices of international parliamentarianism. It would be an approach in which moral values were given their true place, and it would thus be devoid of the illusion that we are somehow virtuous when we profess to speak in the name of morality and sinful when we confess to the possession of interests and aspirations of our own. It would face up to, and attempt to alleviate, the precariousness now involved in the state of our economic exchanges with the outside world. Finally, it would recognize that the respect of others for us must rest upon a true understanding of the advantages of friendly intercourse with us as well as on an awareness that these advantages can and will be forfeited where they are not reciprocated. In general, this approach would, I hope, involve a firm and unapologetic insistence on respect for our national dignity, not just as something we owe to ourselves, but as something we owe to our friends, to our responsibilities, to the sincerity of our convictions, to our own ultimate possibilities for world usefulness.

I am afraid that some of this may have an unpleasant ring, contrasting unfavorably with the cheery good will we all like to radiate when we talk about foreign affairs. I am sorry for this. I think I should emphasize, in conclusion, lest there be any misunderstanding, that I do not wish ever to see the conduct of this nation in its foreign relations animated by anything else than decency, generosity, moderation, and consideration for others. I hope no government will ever approach us in a similar spirit and be permitted to go away disappointed. If I did not believe that, despite all our national failings, our existence as a great nation was by

and large beneficial to the civilization of which we are
a part, if I did not believe that our purposes as a nation were on balance worthy ones, which can be pursued and achieved without injury to any other people,
I would not feel we were entitled to take the attitude
I have suggested this evening. As it is, I do.

III. The Problem of
Soviet Power

WE NOW COME TO THE SECOND of those planes of international reality which I mentioned in the first of these lectures. In doing so we find ourselves face to face with something which is not only the greatest and most urgent and most complex of our present problems of national policy but represents unquestionably the greatest test of statesmanship that our country has ever faced. I am referring here to the problem of Soviet power.

This is too vast a subject for any comprehensive and reasoned analysis in a single evening. All I can hope to do is to remind you of some facts about the problem that seem to me worth bearing in mind, and then to make a few general comments on the most widely discussed concepts as to how we might deal with it.

The first fact to which I should like to invite attention is a geopolitical one, important to all thinking about the Soviet problem. It is this. In a day when large-scale warfare has become a matter of highly complicated and expensive weapons and of central control over great masses of manpower, military strength on a major scale, and particularly strength of an amphibious nature, capable of reaching our homeland and disputing our power within it, can be produced only in a limited number of parts of the globe: in those regions where major industrial power, enjoying adequate access to raw materials, is combined with large reserves of educated and technically skilled manpower. Our own North American community constitutes one such center of military-industrial strength. There are only four others in the world. They are all in the Northern Hemisphere. Two of them, England and Japan, lie off the shores of the Eurasian land mass and belong to the insular and maritime portion of the globe, of which we Americans are also a part. The other two have their seat in the interior of the Eurasian land mass. One of these last two is made up of Germany and the industrial regions immediately contiguous to Germany—the Rhineland, Silesia, Bohemia, and Austria. It is dependent largely on the metallurgical resources of the Rhine Valley, Silesia, and the Alps. The other is represented by the Soviet Union proper, and is similarly dependent on the association of the coal of the Donets Basin and western Siberia with the iron ore and light metals of the Urals and the energetics resources of the Volga-Caspian Basin. I repeat, nowhere outside these five areas can military-industrial strength be produced in this world today on what we might call the grand scale.

One of the happy circumstances of our life is that whatever may be our differences with Britain, her people are thoroughly conscious, I am sure, of the manner in which fate has bound their security with ours. What we are concerned with here, fortunately, is not just Britain as an island, but Britain as the nucleus of a great political and economic system, worldwide in its ramifications, and sharing in overwhelming degree our own world interests. Surely, with any reasonable degree of good will and understanding, we need never fear that Britain will be our enemy. I earnestly hope that a similar situation now prevails with respect to the Japanese, whose geographic situation in the Pacific is analogous to that of the British in the Atlantic. I think we have grounds for such a hope.

That leaves the relationship between Germany and Russia at the heart of our security problem, in the physical sense.

This, I repeat, is a crude concept. There are many qualifying elements in any such simple breakdown of our world security problem. It does not mean that other parts of the world are not important. They are, for various weighty reasons. But it does mean that the danger of Soviet expansionism is not always the same everywhere, regardless of geographic locale. China, for example, is not one of these five key areas; her resources do not nearly come up to this class. And it means that the heart of our problem is to prevent the gathering together of the military-industrial potential of the entire Eurasian land mass under a single power threatening to the interests of the insular and maritime portions of the globe.

The second fact I wish to note has to do with the

physical and military power of the Soviet regime. Prior to 1939 the military strength of Russia, while formidable in certain areas and for certain purposes, was not of such a nature that it appeared as any great immediate threat to the security of central and western Europe. If today that can no longer be said, this is something that must be attributed primarily to the fact that the Soviets have come into control of the physical and technical and manpower resources of the Baltic states, of eastern Germany, and of the satellite countries of eastern Europe.

This development has altered the relationship of Russian strength to central and western European strength in two ways. In the positive sense it has directly enhanced, and quite considerably so, the technological and industrial foundations of Soviet military strength, by adding to it many of the resources of these other countries. In the negative sense it has made more difficult the restoration of any countervailing strength in western and central Europe. These military and political positions in the heart of central Europe and in the Manchurian-Korean area, gained by the Russians through their military advance at the end of the war, gave the Kremlin actual control over a portion of the resources required for any full restoration of German and Japanese power, and thus placed it in a favorable position to hamper and delay the re-growth of that power. In addition—and this is a fact of greatest importance—the occupation of eastern Germany has given to the Soviet Union an area of military deployment in the heart of Europe that serves to overcome the barrier of communications-poor territory from Narva to Bessarabia behind which the main Russian forces were confined before 1939, and which constituted one of the main defenses of central and western Europe.

The result has been that the balance of power in Europe and Asia in conventional weapons has been greatly and seriously altered to Russia's advantage. How much China has affected this, I do not know. For that reason I have not included China in the calculation. Naturally, her political association with the Soviet Union has brought many advantages to the Kremlin. The use of the Chinese as puppet forces to assume the burden of opposing us on the Korean Peninsula was only the most conspicuous of these. But it also has brought many disadvantages. China is distinctly a resources-poor country. In the long run she will be in many ways a drain on the industrial resources of the Soviet Union. How the pluses and minuses will finally tot up, I simply do not know. I would warn against all sweeping assumptions on this score.

This leaves us with the conclusion that so far as military potential is concerned, the inordinate position of relative strength recently enjoyed by Russia has been largely the result of the temporary prostration of Germany and Japan in consequence of the recent World War, and the accretions to the Soviet military orbit which came about through the course of military operations in the final phases of the war.

The Problem of Soviet Power

The next fact we must note is the congenital and deep-seated hostility of the Soviet regime to the older and larger countries of the western world, and particularly to the United States. There has been much argument as to what caused this hostility: whether it was a preconception of the communist movement or whether it was something provoked by western policies toward the Soviet regime in the years of its infancy. Actually, both factors enter in, but the more important of the two has been by far the ideological prejudice entertained by the Soviet leaders long before they seized power in Petrograd in 1917. If there is anyone who doubts the accuracy of this judgment, I would suggest he read the pronouncements of the Soviet leaders during the period just before and after their accession to power in 1917.

Later the responsibilities of power began to render it convenient for the Soviet leaders to have an external enemy by whose menacing presence their own excesses and cruelties could be explained and justified. In the 'thirties they actually had such an enemy—two of them, in fact: the Germans and the Japanese—both quite genuine, so genuine that they served with some degree of plausibility as excuses for the bloody purges that marked the middle of that decade. But when World War II eliminated these real enemies, a fictitious one had to be found, and we were it.

We had every qualification for being cast in such a role. By our insistence on remaining in Germany and Austria and controlling Japan, by stiffening Europe with Marshall Plan aid, and by defending the political integrity of South Korea, we prevented that complete sweep of dominant Soviet influence over Europe and Asia which was Stalin's initial postwar hope. By keeping freedom alive in the immediate proximity of the Soviet-occupied areas, we complicated the consolidation of communist control there and maintained, in effect, a constant threat to the security of Soviet power. For there is no influence more dangerous and disruptive to the totalitarian state than the knowledge on the part of its subjects that somewhere else in the world there still is such a thing as freedom, and the faint, stubborn hope that they, too, might some day enjoy it.

For all these reasons we must recognize Soviet hostility as something reflecting a deep historical and political logic; and we must not be moved by the silly suggestions, recurring from time to time in western opinion, that this hostility might easily be made to disappear if some of our statesmen were to make themselves personally agreeable to the Soviet leaders. This is a hostility that will not be caused to disappear by either the cocktail or the vodka glass.

The existence of this hostility often leads people to hasty and erroneous conclusions as to Soviet intentions. Here we must be careful to avoid confusion. Hostility is one thing; intentions another.

As many of you already know, I have never seen any evidence that the Soviet leaders have at any time since World War II (or before, for that matter) desired a general war between the Soviet Union and the major capitalist powers, or looked to such a war as a likely means of achieving their objectives. I believe they have considered that a general war of this sort, even if successful in the initial military stages, would be too risky, too expensive, and would involve too much in the way of sudden assumption of inordinate political responsibility over conquered areas to be a hopeful device of Soviet policy. The Soviet leaders are not like many of us; they do not suppose that military victory solves all problems; they know that it is only a beginning and not an end.

Their ideology *does* tell them, however, that the capitalist powers, and above all the United States, will eventually be inclined to seek a war with the Soviet Union as a way out of the political frustrations and difficulties to which capitalism is supposed to be subjected in ever-increasing degree. They think, in other words, that we will be driven by the logic of our social system to *want* a war with them, and to seek it to the best of our ability, within the limits of normal political and military prudence.

But they comfort themselves with two reflections. So far as the nightmarish possibilities of atomic weapons are concerned, they believe these can be, and may well be, cancelled out by the prospect of retaliation. In other words, they doubt that these weapons will ever be used. Secondly, they feel that before we can arrive at the point where a preventive war would be a realistic possibility for us, we will be decisively weakened by what they call the "contradictions" of the capitalistic world. By this they mean every sort of internal division and difference within the western family itself. These internal difficulties will, they hope, make it impossible in practice for us to launch the war we might abstractedly desire. And these difficulties can, they feel, be intensified by clever tactics and propaganda from the communist side.

Of all the hopes in the Soviet breast, the most businesslike and serious ones, the ones most formidable to us, center around this prospect for sowing disunity everywhere in the western camp, and particularly in every relationship that has anything to do with western strength. That means disunity within our own country as between classes, and races, and outlooks. It means disunity between ourselves and our allies. It means the disruption of the confidence of others in us, of our confidence in others. It means, above all, the disruption of our confidence in ourselves. Here—not in elaborate blueprints and timetables of military conquest, but in hopes for the demoralization and disintegration of our world—lies the thing that we are really entitled to describe as the major Soviet design.

It is here, of course, that the foreign communist parties come in. I think it important to recognize and to bear in mind their allotted role in the Soviet scheme of things. Ever since its inception, the Soviet regime has had, in the form of the communist parties and communist stooge groups in various other countries, an arsenal of political weapons which it could use as supplementary instruments for the achievement of its policy aims. It is important to note that in no instance did the Soviet leaders themselves actually create the basic circumstances that made possible the existence and effectiveness of these weapons. It may be said of the non-communist world, in Asia as in Europe, that it was in part ripe to be abused and exploited in the way that Moscow abuses and exploits it. It had illnesses which provided the opportunities for the bacilli of communist destruction. In Europe the illness consisted of the weariness and bewilderment of the peoples following two phenomenally destructive world wars, of the unsettling effects of technological change on a mellow and tradition-bound civilization, and finally of the fact that modern democracy is by nature vulnerable to having exploited against it the very liberties and privileges by which it lives. In Asia the illness lay in the development of the colonial problem, in the general social unrest, and above all in the receptiveness of millions of people to ideological clichés that promised them, at one and the same time, an alternative to the acceptance of the hated ideologies of the western capitalist powers and a sort of a magic short-cut to the coveted emoluments of industrial and material progress. Everywhere, and at all times, communist success has been mainly a function, almost an automatic function, of weakness, illness, and irrealism elsewhere.

Fortunately there seem to have been limits almost everywhere to the sort of weakness that did constitute an invitation to communism. One of the most striking things about the whole phenomenon of international,

The Problem of Soviet Power

Moscow-controlled communism has been the minor degree of political success it has generally enjoyed. I know of no country in the world where the communists have ever been supported by a real electoral majority. I believe the highest vote they ever got was a 38 per-cent vote in Czechoslovakia. In most countries with any reasonable degree of political health, the number of their followers generally rarely exceeds five or six percent. This percentage undoubtedly represents in large part a certain margin of human nature, so con-stituted that it lends itself congenitally to exploita-tion by outside forces against the society of which it is a part. Where communism has assumed larger dimen-sions, as today in France and Italy, this has been the result of deep-seated internal maladjustments from which the communists have simply been able to profit, mostly through their ruthless and effective organiza-tional talents. It has not been, or at least it has been in only very minor degree, the reflection of any suc-cess of communist ideas *per se*. The belief, frequently expressed in this country, that there has been in re-cent years some sort of a triumph of Soviet propaganda is simply devoid of substance. The fact is that the ideological attraction of Soviet communism has de-clined generally since the mid-'thirties. Its ideas have been increasingly exposed as the postulates of an ex-tremely crude and rigid pseudo-science, outdated in its terms of reference, plainly wrong in its most im-portant assumptions, overtaken everywhere by the real course of events. The prestige of Soviet power has

73

come increasingly to rest simply on its ruthless organizational efficiency, its rigid discipline, and the impressive quality of its military posture. But these are not the same thing as ideas.

In addition to this, we must remember that in many instances the preservation of the disciplinary bonds by which these groups of foreign communists have been held in subjection by Moscow has depended precisely on their remaining what they were: weak opposition groups, with very little real indigenous support, extensively dependent on inspiration, encouragement, and disciplinary stiffening from without. Moscow has long recognized this, and has realized that if these parties were to grow into majority parties, or anything like it, and then actually to come into power in their respective countries, their dependence on Moscow would be greatly reduced and Tito-ism, in one form or another, would become a virtual inevitability everywhere except under the direct shadow of Soviet military power.

For this reason it is quite erroneous to assume that what Moscow is after is to have all these foreign communist parties seize power at the earliest possible moment. The effect of this would probably be only to see many of them lost as political instruments of the Kremlin. But Moscow desires to retain them as instruments. It wants to use them for the reduction of competing political strength, for the sowing of discord and distrust among other countries, for the weakening of political and military potential elsewhere, for the sabotaging of resistance to the Kremlin's own foreign policies.

In the light of this fact it is interesting to note that, with the single exception of China, nowhere in the world has there actually been any spread of communist power in the last thirty years, other than in areas where it was installed by Soviet bayonets and where the Soviet military power could continue, with ease and convenience, to breathe down its neck. The one exception, as I say, was China. And that is precisely why the relationship of China to the Kremlin today, despite all outward appearances, is an uneasy and unstable one, not fully clarified, not fully comfortable.

These, then, are the facts about Soviet power I thought we should note by way of introduction to this discussion. With these facts in mind, let us turn again to the problems of our own national policy.

You have all followed, to one degree or another, the great debate about policy toward the Soviet Union that has dominated our public discussions in these recent years. Let me attempt to summarize the nature of this debate.

We all recognize, I think, that the present bloated state of the Soviet empire represents, primarily for the geopolitical reasons I have already outlined, an unhealthy situation and a danger to everyone concerned. We all recognize that any further expansion of Soviet power would represent a still greater danger. Our differences relate only to what it is that we ought to do in the light of these two recognitions.

First, there is the difference of opinion as to where we should place our hopes for an actual reduction of Soviet power and influence: whether on the operation of natural forces within the Soviet Union or on the application of pressure from outside. That is the question of *liberation*. Secondly, there is the question as to how to prevent the process of Soviet expansion from going further. That is the question of *containment*.

Let me emphasize: these concepts are *not* alternatives, and the argument is *not* about whether one or the other is most desirable. I know of no one in our ranks, including myself, who would not like to see the area of Soviet power and influence reduced. Therefore, we are all in favor of "liberation." Conversely, I know of no one in our ranks who thinks it would be desirable that Soviet power should expand still farther. Therefore, we are all in favor of "containment." Our differences concern only the means by which each of these objectives is to be sought.

Let me turn first to the one that seems to me to afford the most dangerous possibilities for error and misjudgment—namely, liberation. And let me make myself quite plain.

The retraction of Soviet power from its present bloated and unhealthy limits is essential to the stability of world relationships. To bring it about must be a cardinal aim of western policy. But the term "liberation" can mean many things. It is one of those vague clichés the very currency of which depends on their imprecision. And as the term is most frequently used in this country, and particularly by those who regard themselves as its strongest protagonists, it seems to me to have two main implications. First, it implies the violent overthrow of Soviet power in either all or a portion of the present Soviet orbit. Second, it implies that this overthrow should constitute an active aim of western, and particularly American, policy—that the main impulse to it, in other words, should come from without and from us, rather than from within the Soviet orbit itself.

Now I think we must recognize, first of all, that if this is what we have in mind, and if we mean it seriously—that is, if we are not just indulging in fine phrases—then we are talking about a path of policy which, if pushed far enough, would by every law of probability lead ultimately to war. The Soviet leaders are not going to dismantle their power in eastern Europe for the love of our beautiful eyes, or because we set out to huff and to puff and to blow their house in. Their power does not rest on the consent of the governed; and it is not of the sort that would be easily shaken by propaganda to the subject peoples, even if there were effective things that we could say. The very attempt to shake it by external action is exactly the thing that would make it impossible for the Soviet leaders to yield any portion of it except under the pressure of war.

You cannot expect a group of totalitarian rulers to

step down from the scene of world history and to acquiesce in the destruction of their political system for the sake of the preservation of peace. These people have no future outside of their own political power. There is no place for them to go. Their chances for personal survival would be minimal if that power were really weakened. Let no one think that they could give up a portion of it by way of submission to some foreign ultimatum, and still retain the remainder, unaffected. One of the great realities of political life is the cumulative nature of all political change, the factor of momentum in human affairs, the dynamic character of all alterations in political prestige. The Soviet leaders know this; and it explains why they are sensitive about yielding anything under pressure, even at the remotest ends of their empire.

I can conceive that Soviet power will some day recede from its present exposed positions, just as it has already receded in Finland and Yugoslavia and northern Iran. But I can conceive of this happening only precisely in the event that the vital prestige of Soviet power is not too drastically and abruptly engaged in the process, in the event that the change is permitted to come gradually and inconspicuously and as the result of compulsions resident within the structure of Soviet power itself, not created externally in the form of threats or ultimata or patent intrigues from outside.

If the transition cannot be eased over in this way, then I see little likelihood of its occurring at all without leading ultimately to a general armed conflict. And I would like to emphasize that any war that might appear to be the consequence of our own policies would proceed under the gravest of disadvantages. It would bring dismay and despair to people all over the world who would like to think of themselves as our friends and to look to us for world leadership. It would almost certainly disrupt our alliances and jeopardize the enjoyment of the advantages of them, an extremely important consideration from the standpoint of the prospects for sheer military success. It would come to the Russian people, and possibly to those other peoples for whose liberation some of us are so concerned, as an appalling and unjustified injury—an injury not just to the communist leaders but to the subject peoples themselves—arousing every spark of patriotism of which they are capable, and establishing the communist authorities in the most favorable possible political position as leaders in the defense of the peoples against aggressive attack. Millions of Americans, I am sure, could take part in such a war only at the expense of the most tortured doubts as to whether this new calamity to civilization had really been necessary, whether there was really no other way to work out the problem. And all of this would be aside from the question of the destruction that might be wrought on our own American territory in the use of atomic weapons.

In addition to this, I think it necessary and pertinent to recognize that any war fought in the name of liberation could not and would not be fully successful, either militarily or politically, precisely for the reason that its aims would be too sweeping, too ambitious, and too total. People have become accustomed to saying that the day of limited wars is over. I would submit that the truth is exactly the opposite: that the day of total wars has passed, and that from now on limited military operations are the only ones that could conceivably serve any coherent purpose.

Russia, let us remember, cannot be wholly occupied. No matter how successful military operations might be, there would presumably always come a point at which you would have to enter into communication with your communist adversaries again and to arrive at some sort of realistic arrangement with them. There could be no expectation, here, of "unconditional surrender" along the lines of the precedents of the last two world wars.

Even in those areas that might be "liberated," there would be the question of civil affairs, the question of some new political authority to replace the old. Are we prepared for that? Do we have such alternatives in our pocket in all conceivable cases? In the case of the Soviet Union, at any rate, I doubt that we do. And I shudder at the responsibility we would have assumed, if we were to occupy such areas, and yet had no vigorous indigenous political movement to support us. That is the position in which we found ourselves during the intervention in Russia and Siberia in 1917–18, and if there is anyone who doubts the reality of these reflections, let him read the sorry history of those ill-conceived ventures. It is extraordinary how rarely it seems to occur to Americans that every victory is a responsibility, and that there are limits to the responsibilities we should invite upon ourselves.

The upshot of what I am saying is that in my view this Soviet problem, while a great one, is not suitably to be resolved by war. I do not mean to argue this point tonight, but I think you would all find on reflection that there is a deep general reality involved in this, and that major war, deliberately undertaken, cannot by its very nature serve effectively to promote positive and constructive aims of society. Major war can be at best the lesser of two evils, a terrible and heavy price paid in order to avoid the necessity of paying one still more terrible and still more heavy; but then it must be a defensive war, forced upon us, accepted reluctantly and with heavy heart.

I would like to be able to leave the question of war at this point, for it is a prospect from which we must learn to look away if we are to discover the true avenues for the alleviation of our problems with the Russians, but I am afraid that it cannot be left without a further word, addressed to those people who have a tendency to say: How can you stand there and talk quietly about all these things when you know that the Russians have the Bomb, and that they may at this very moment have the capacity for destroying our cities? Is there, these people ask, anything else that counts, anything else worth talking about, in this whole Soviet problem?

There is no use arguing with the premises of these people. They may exaggerate many details, but even that does not affect the main issue. Of course the day of absolute security is gone, if it was ever here. Of course other people either have it in their power today, or will have it soon, to lay waste to our cities, if the devil possesses them. I still find in all this no reason for any morbid excitement. Is there anything surprising in any of it? Did people really suppose that in a world of atomic realities we Americans could live forever in the sole possession of a sort of sorcerer's charm by which everyone else would always be inferior to us militarily and bound to defer to our will in a pinch?

The question is not what people *could* conceivably do. We are all of us, in personal life, at the mercy of crackpots, maniacs, even of wild drivers on the highways. Such security as we have in personal life rests on what people actually do, in the law of averages, rather than on what they could do. Fortunately a push-button attack on this country actually makes little more sense from the standpoint of our adversaries than would a similar attack by ourselves on someone else. It would serve no sound political purpose. It would not really assure to them the sort of quiet and cautious expansion of power that they are seeking. It would only mess things up badly in this world, for everyone concerned, themselves included.

Besides, there is always the factor of retaliation. If we retain a prudent measure of the capacity to retaliate and a reasonable dispersal of the facilities requisite thereto, there is no reason to suppose that anyone is going to find it in his interest to destroy our country out of a blue sky.

People will say: yes, but we cannot depend on this; we cannot depend on others to be sane and rational. To some small extent, of course, this is true. But I think great political regimes are apt to have quite a rational comprehension of their own most vital and immediate military interests. In the Soviet regime, in particular, I have never detected any suicidal tendencies; and I will do its leaders the justice to say that while I think them very misguided people and have no high opinion of their intentions with regard to this country, I do not suspect them of any desire to wreak upon others some fearful measure of destruction just for destruction's own sake, apart from any coherent political or social purpose. These people are not ogres; they are just badly misguided and twisted human beings, deeply involved in the predicaments that invariably attend the exercise of great power.

Of course there is danger in our contemporary world, but when has human life ever been without danger? The sort of jitters apparent in a portion of our press and public is not only unworthy of the traditions of our country, it does not even do justice to the way most of us would behave if danger were to become a reality. And the worst thing about it is that it actually increases the seriousness of our situation. If we all sit quietly in our little boat and address ourselves to the process of navigation, I doubt that it will tip over; but if we all leap up from our seats and go rushing around grabbing each other by the lapel and screaming, "Why don't you *do* something about it?" we will be on the surest way to making it capsize.

The weapons of mass destruction have to be borne in mind as one of the great and sorry realities of our day. We cannot rule out the possibility of war, for wars can arise from many constellations of circumstance; and similarly we cannot rule out the possibility that these horrible weapons may some day be used. For this contingency we must make the most realistic dispositions we can, but we must not be carried away by these dispositions to the point where we neglect the cultivation of the other possibilities. There is also the possibility that there will be no general war. And there is always the further possibility that even if there is a war, it may prove the part of prudence for us all to restrict ourselves either to the more conventional weapons or to a more conventional use of the unconventional ones. For this, too, we must be prepared. It is for this reason that I would fail to comprehend any policy that did not preserve a balance between conventional weapons and the weapons of mass destruction, and especially one that staked our world position on the power of weapons we ourselves, in the final event, might or might not find it prudent to use. The sooner we can learn to cultivate the weapons of mass destruction solely for their deterrent value, the sooner we can get away from what is called the principle of "first use" of such weapons, the sooner we can free ourselves from the false mathematics involved in the assumption that security is a matter of the number of people you can kill with a single weapon, the better off, in my opinion, we will be.

So much for liberation, for preventative war, and for the atomic bomb. We are left, as usual, with the other side of our problem, the old and familiar side which many people find it so distasteful to talk about: the side of "containment." There seems to be a theory, especially since the Korean war, that this is a matter of preventing armies from crossing frontiers for aggressive purposes. I find little to substantiate this view. Certainly in every immediate sense it is a matter of preventing other peoples from committing the naive and fateful folly of permitting the reins of government to be seized within their respective countries by elements that accept the disciplinary authority of Moscow. And this, as you will readily perceive, is not primarily a matter of Soviet policy but a matter of policy for the non-communist peoples themselves.

I recognize that what I am saying is precisely the opposite of another view which would hold Moscow formally responsible for all communist activity everywhere, and punishable for every attempt of a communist minority to seize power. I am sorry to have to say that I do not think that things are quite this simple. I pointed out earlier that communist penetration in the non-communist world is not solely a matter of Soviet initiative or support, but contains a very important component of local origin, in the weaknesses and illnesses of a given society. Moreover, Soviet officials have a point when they remind us that they do not challenge the right of any other government to deal as it will with its communist minority, and do not protest diplomatically when such minorities are treated sternly and rendered ineffective through police action. The literal physical destruction of the German communist party by Hitler in the 'thirties was not only *not* the subject of any diplomatic protests from Moscow to Berlin, but was actually accompanied by a series of diplomatic approaches from the Soviet side that led eventually to the amiable arrangement of the Nazi-Soviet Non-Aggression Pact. Thus Moscow does not dispute the right of others to take whatever steps they wish to take in order to control their own communist elements. But where they are unwilling to take those steps, Moscow is not prepared to do it for them. Nor can the Moscow leaders properly be expected to see to it that their views never, by any chance, commend themselves to people elsewhere.

I realize full well that this is not all there is to it: that there are training schools for subversion behind the Iron Curtain, that there is conspiracy, that there are secret agents and spies, and all of this to no good purpose. But underlying all this, and making it all possible, is the fact that there are great areas of softness and vulnerability in the non-communist world, areas which it lies wholly in the competence of non-communist authority to remove. If certain of these areas could be removed, there would be, I think, no further expansion of Soviet power. If they are not removed, our fortunes—the fortunes of all people who look for a continued unfolding of the process of civilization and for a continued growth in the dignity of the human spirit—are unquestionably going to suffer. But we cannot look to Moscow, which did not create these soft spots, to remove them. Our problem is not that simple. We will have to continue to search for other solutions.

Thus the problem of containment is basically a problem of the reactions of people within the non-communist world. It is true that this condition depends upon the maintenance by ourselves and our allies, at all times, of an adequate defense posture, designed to guard against misunderstandings and to give confidence and encouragement to the weak and the faint-hearted. But so long as that posture is maintained, the things that need most to be done to prevent the further expansion of Soviet power are not, so far as we are concerned, things we can do directly in our relations with the Soviet Government; they are things we must do in our relations with the peoples of the non-communist world.

On the other hand—and this is the final thought I would like to leave in your minds this evening—it is my belief that these very same things are precisely the most useful things we can do in the interest of the eventual greater freedom of the peoples now behind the Curtain. Whatever we do that serves to bring hope

and encouragement and self-confidence to peoples outside the Soviet orbit has a similar effect on the peoples
inside, and constitutes the most potent sort of argument for prudence and reasonableness on the part of
the Soviet leaders. To the extent we are able to realize
this, we will understand that containment and liberation are only two sides of the same coin, and both part
of a greater problem—the problem of how the behavior of this nation is to be so shaped as to command
the hope and confidence of all those who wish us well
and the respect of all those who do not, whichever side
of the Curtain they may be on.

Permit me now to say a few words in conclusion. I
fear that the points I have touched on this evening may
have seemed disjointed and without relation to each
other, but I think that if stacked up side by side they
do constitute a way of looking at the Soviet problem,
and one which is not quite so depressing as some of the
others now current in our country. Let me recapitulate
them.

Soviet hostility to us is bitter and deep, but it does
not mean that the Soviet leaders want war.

The communist parties in the free countries are a
nuisance and an impertinence, but they are largely a
reflection of weakness within those countries themselves and they need not represent a mortal danger to
any country that wishes to keep its own house in order.

The weapons of mass destruction are a sad and
dangerous fact of our contemporary life, but they need
not necessarily ever be used.

The Problem of Soviet Power

The geographic over-extension of Soviet power is a serious and unhealthy anomaly, and needs desperately to be remedied, but there is no sudden and drastic and direct way of seeking to remedy it that would not draw down upon us all, friends, enemies, and Americans alike, new miseries and confusions far worse than those we would be concerned to overcome.

In all of this I see no reason for jitters, for panic, or for melodramatic actions. I do see reasons for hard work, for sober thinking, for a great deliberateness of statesmanship, for a high degree of national self-discipline, and for the cultivation of an atmosphere of unity and mutual confidence among our own people.

The greatest danger presented to us by Soviet policy is still its attempt to promote internecine division and conflict within our system of alliances and within our own body politic. But this is something we have it in our power to counteract by the quality of our leadership and the tone of our own national life generally. If these were what they should be, they would radiate themselves to the world at large, and the warmth of that radiation would not only represent the best means of frustrating the design for further Soviet expansion— it would also be the best means of helping the peoples behind the Iron Curtain to recover their freedom. For you will all recall the Aesopian fable about the competition between the Sun and the North Wind to see which of them could make the traveler remove his cloak. Well, the traveler is the phenomenon of Soviet power. The cloak is that zone of inordinate power and influence in eastern Europe and elsewhere with which it has tried to shelter its own inner sanctum. And you will all recall that it was not by the direct huffing and puffing of the North Wind, but by the gentle indirection of the Sun that the stubborn traveler was at last induced to remove his cloak.

IV. The Unifying Factor

I AM AFRAID THAT in the last two of these lectures I found it necessary to speak primarily about things we ought *not* to do rather than about things we *ought* to do in our foreign relations. I hope tonight to correct in some measure the resulting deficiency and to indicate to you certain of what seem to me to be the more hopeful and constructive possibilities of American foreign policy. But before I enter on this task, there are one or two things I would like to add, by way of afterthought, to what I said last night with regard to the problem of Soviet power. I am afraid that if I do not do this there will be certain serious gaps in the pattern of the Soviet problem I left in your minds.

You will recall that I hinted at the possibility that the changes in the Soviet order which we would like to see occur—above all, the retraction of the limits of Soviet power and influence to something more normal and more compatible with the peace of the world—might conceivably come as the result of the workings of internal forces within the structure of Soviet power, with only an indirect encouragement from ourselves and the rest of the outside world. I know that this intimation will be challenged by some people who do not believe in the possibility of such change, or who fear that it will not occur soon enough to be of any significance to us. It is about this attitude that I would like to say a few words.

It seems to me that in the field of international affairs one should never be so sure of his analysis of the future as to permit it to become a source of complete despair. The greatest law of human history is its unpredictability. Here, in this Soviet problem, we have the greatest possible need for the broad historical perspective. There has never been a country that was not susceptible to change. Evolution occurs everywhere, if only as a response to change in physical conditions—alterations in population and resources and technology. Does anyone really suppose that a nation could undergo so violent a process of technological change as has marked the Soviet Union in these past decades and yet remain unaffected in its social and political life? Or is it held that the Bolshevik Revolution of 1917 brought into being a political system so far-sighted, so comprehensive, so well-designed, that it can bear without modification, indefinitely, the weight of any conceivable degree of physical and technological change? It would be an ill omen for us all if we were obliged to admit this. For certainly, only a political system magnificently attuned to the inner needs of man could meet this supreme test.

Actually, history has already belied this fear. There has already been change in the Soviet orbit. There was a great change from Leninism to Stalinism. There is a change in process today from Stalinism to something else; and the fact that this "something else" is not fully clear to us is not a proof that it does not exist, or that it will not be something closer to the requirements of international stability than what we have known hitherto in the Soviet system. It is my impression that there must already be in progress, in the relations between Moscow and the various satellite governments, a certain subtle evolution, the effects of which may as yet be in no way visible, but which may nevertheless be of greatest importance for the development of the Soviet program as a whole.

If there is any great lesson we Americans need to learn with regard to the methodology of foreign policy, it is that we must be gardeners and not mechanics in our approach to world affairs. We must come to think of the development of international life as an organic and not a mechanical process. We must realize that we did not create the forces by which this process operates. We must learn to take these forces for what they are and to induce them to work with us and for us by influencing the environmental stimuli to which they are subjected, but to do this gently and patiently, with understanding and sympathy, not trying to force growth by mechanical means, not tearing the plants up by the roots when they fail to behave as we wish them to. The forces of nature will generally be on the side of him who understands them best and respects them most scrupulously. We do not need to insist, as the communists do, that change in the camp of *our* adversaries can come only by violence. Our concept of the possibility of improvement in the condition of mankind is not predicated, as is that of the communists, on the employment of violence as a means to its real- ization. If our outlook on life is, as we believe it to be, more closely attuned to the real nature of man than that of our communist adversaries, then we can afford to be patient and even occasionally to suffer reverses, placing our confidence in the longer and deeper work- ings of history.

I would also like to add a few words of reinforce- ment to what I said at the conclusion of last night's lecture about the effects on the Soviet orbit of our own behavior here at home and in our relations generally with the non-communist countries. There seems to be an assumption among some of our people that the Rus- sian communists and their people take note of us only when we do something that affects them directly. I would like to warn strongly against this assumption. Don't think that we are not watched at all times with most careful and anxious eyes from the other side of the Iron Curtain. Don't think that the resulting ob- servations do not have the most far-reaching repercus- sions on the hopes and fears and calculations both of the rulers and the ruled in the Soviet camp, and con- sequently on the entire trend of the political relation- ship between them. When we make fools of ourselves and mess up our own affairs and bring dismay and anxiety into the hearts of those who would like to be our friends and our allies, this is reflected at once by a new birth of false hopes and arrogance in the minds of those who rule the roost in Moscow. When, on the other hand, we speak with a voice—or better, act with a voice—that carries courage and determination and inner conviction to the world at large, believe me, it is heard by millions and millions of people, and every heart that cares anything for freedom thrills to it, and those who hear it do not ask by what precise military calculations we propose to bring Soviet power to an end or on what day this is supposed to happen. They are wiser than many of us in this respect; and they know that just because one cannot predict the precise steps by which courage and faith earn their victories in this world, the power of these qualities is nonetheless formidable for that fact.

Finally, while I am still dealing in after-thoughts, I would like to say a few words about the particular problem we have in those specific areas that are today most threatened by indigenous communist pressures; for it is there that the attention of our people and the world is riveted just at this moment, and I fear that any presentation that did not contain a specific reference to them would be incomplete.

So far as Indo-China itself is concerned, which is eighty percent of the problem today in the immediate sense, I think there is little to be gained at this moment by any attempt to master-mind our government's actions, day by day, from the outside. This is an incredibly complex and baffling situation. We are now in it up to the hilt. The time has passed when any back seat driving can do any good. Our government is obviously making a concentrated and determined effort to come to grips with the problem. We can only wish them well and give them our confidence and support. There are times when, having elected a government, we will be best advised to let it govern and to let it speak for us as it will in the councils of the nations.

But there are a few considerations with regard to the general problem of communism in Asia which might be worth noting at this point. It is here, above all, that we must avoid the fallacy that we are dealing with some threat of military aggression comparable to that which faced the world when Hitler put his demands on the Poles in 1939. Military aggression can never be ruled out entirely as a possibility, but it is not the most urgent and likely of the possibilities with which we have to reckon. We are dealing here in large measure with tendencies and states of mind which, however misguided and however befuddled by deceptions practiced from outside, are nevertheless basically the reflections of wholly real and even profound indigenous conditions, and would not be caused to disappear even in the unthinkable event that Moscow could be threatened or bludgeoned into telling them to do so. We are dealing here with great emotional forces, and not with rational reactions.

We could perhaps exploit these forces with relative ease, as the communists do, if we had the cynicism and the shamelessness and the heartlessness to do it. We, too, could promise men things we know to be illusory. We, too, could hold out short-term advantages as baits for a long-term enslavement. We, too, could incite hatreds and fan suspicions and try to strike profit from the workings of bitterness and blind fury.

But we Americans are not set up for this type of exploitation, either morally or politically. This being the case, there are limits to what we can expect to accomplish; and I would be foolish to encourage you to believe that there are any simple or sure solutions to these baffling problems. There is no certain means by which other people can be prevented from following the Pied Piper to their destruction if their childishness and lack of realism are of this extraordinary order.

Some of these troublesome situations have existed for a long time. I can conceive that they may have to exist for a long time still. We would do well to remind ourselves here, again, that just because the solutions of problems are not visible at any particular time does not mean that those problems will never be alleviated or confined to tolerable dimensions. History has a way of changing the very terms in which problems operate and of leaving them, in the end, unsolved to be sure, yet strangely deflated of their original meaning and their importance.

I do not mean to say that we have no possibilities at all for influencing the situation in these uncertain areas, or that we should not make the effort. But I would like to point out that this does not mean many of the things that Americans seem to think it means. It does not mean that we should breathe down the necks of these peoples and smother them with our influence and attention. It does not mean that we should give them the impression that they have to choose between the Russians and ourselves. It does not mean that we should deluge them with words and with great numbers of American officials and visitors. None of these things is necessarily useful; all of them can, on occasion, be harmful.

We must remember that many people in these countries have, for various reasons, a pathological fear of what they have come to think of as being dominated by the United States. If they are told that they have to choose between the Russians and ourselves, this fills them only with frustration and despair, and paralyzes whatever action they might otherwise be capable of in their own interests. Our propaganda often fails to carry to them because their problems are deep and painful and highly personal, and sometimes there is really nothing we can say to them about themselves, or very little, that comes with tact and good grace from a nation so wealthy and successful as our own. The presence of American officials in large numbers is not always useful, because people in general, and Americans in particular, do not always appear at their best when transplanted to a foreign environment. And the material comforts to which most Americans have become accustomed and to which they cling so tenaciously even when they live abroad, have a tendency to invite envy and contempt rather than admiration when they are sported in the midst of people who do not themselves enjoy them.

Instead of all these things, and instead of the attempt

to appear eager for intimacy and full of helpful suggestions, I think it would be better, as things stand today, if we were to display toward the peoples of these unsettled areas an American personality marked by a very special reserve and dignity, fully prepared to admit that we probably do not have all the answers to their problems, not necessarily demanding that the values of our own civilization should be fully understood and appreciated by others, prepared to recognize the experimental and tentative nature of our own national institutions, requiring of others not that we be liked, or imitated, or admired, but only that we be respected for our seriousness of purpose, our belief in ourselves, and the fundamental reasonableness of our approach. I would hope that there might come a time, as I shall have occasion to explain later this evening, when we would have more than this to say to peoples in Asia and elsewhere. But as things stand today, and as we Americans *are* today, I think we should do well to lay this sort of restraint upon ourselves.

So much for the after-thoughts. Now for the burden of what I should like to say by way of conclusion.

It seems to me evident, from the considerations that have been set forth in the preceding lectures, that in no area of our foreign policy will we be well served, in this coming period, by an approach directed strictly to countering the Soviet threat as a straight military problem. This consideration is valid not only for our relations with the non-communist countries, whose people obviously expect other and more positive things from us; it is also valid from the standpoint of our approach to the communist problem itself in its broader aspects.

Let us remember that the dominant characteristic of our present international situation is the passing of the phenomenon people have called "bipolarity"—a state of affairs that marked the immediate post-hostilities period—and the rise to renewed vigor and importance of the so-called "in-between" countries, particularly our recent enemies, but not only them. We are today in the midst of a transition from a simple to a complex international pattern. Yet many of us seem not to be aware of this.

The test of statesmanship for both the Russians and ourselves in the coming period is going to be the skill with which we are able to adjust to this new situation, and the vision and imagination with which we succeed in shaping new and advantageous relations with the in-between countries, to replace those that have rested, since the recent war, on the abnormal conditions of political subjection in the Russian case, and economic dependence in our own. Here, in application to this new task, a strictly military approach, which attempts to subordinate all other considerations to the balancing of the military equation, will be not only inadequate but downright harmful. For the demands placed on our policy by the rise of these in-between countries to positions of new vitality and importance will often be in direct conflict with the requirements of the perfect and total military posture; and any marked failure on our part to meet these new demands will only be capitalized on at once by the communists within the respective countries; so that by a rigid military approach we will be in danger of losing on the political level more than we gain on the military one. We will be like the man whose exclusive preoccupation with barricading the front door has made it easy for his enemies to enter by the back door.

Now what the in-between countries are looking to us for is not to be taught how to combat communism—however much we may think they need to learn about it—but rather for positive and imaginative suggestions as to how the peaceful future of the world might be shaped and how our own vast economic strength in particular might be so adjusted to the lives of other peoples as to permit a fruitful and mutually profitable interchange, without leading to relationships of political dependence and coercion. But it is not only the more conspicuous of the in-between countries who are looking to us for this; it is all the non-communist countries, in fact, and even all the subject peoples within the communist orbit, who know that their chances of liberation will be best if we Americans are able to develop positive and constructive purposes that serve to place the negative, destructive purposes of communism in the shadows where they belong.

In the larger sense, therefore, it may be said that the problem of world communism is one of those problems which can be dealt with effectively only if you learn to look away from it, not in the sense that you take no precautionary measures with regard to it, but in the sense that you do not permit it to preoccupy your thoughts and your vision but rather insist on the right to proceed with your positive undertakings in spite of it. This is a quality not peculiar to Moscow's communism. Only too often in life we find ourselves beset by demons, sometimes outside ourselves, sometimes within us, who have power over us only so long as they are able to monopolize our attention and lose that power when we refuse to permit ourselves to be diverted and intimidated by them and when we simply go on with the real work we know we have to do. Thus it is with communism; and in this recognition lies, I believe, not only the key to the only successful method of dealing with that particular phenomenon but also the key to a successful global approach to our world problems generally, in this coming period. It is to the possible nature of such a global approach that I would like to devote the remainder of my observations.

Let us attempt, for a moment, to look beyond the problem of Soviet power, at least to the extent that we assume a world with no single political group seriously aspiring to world domination and with no more than what we might call the normal incidence of tension, misunderstanding, and violence. Toward what sort of an ultimate pattern of international relationships would we, in such circumstances, like to see the world community move? And what would be our place in this pattern?

In the first of these lectures I spoke of the original objects of American society and of the modest limited concepts of foreign policy that flowed from them. These concepts still appeal to me strongly. Even today I find them preferable to pretentious and unrealistic ones. But I must confess that I do not think that the original objects from which these concepts flowed are now fully adequate to the present nature of our society, to the significance of our position in the world, and to the responsibilities that rest upon us. I believe, in other words, that we must consciously enlarge the objects of our society in order that they may become commensurate with our present stature as a nation.

You will recall that those objects were initially confined to the cultivation of a certain type of social experiment on our national territory and did not embrace any real sense of responsibility for the trend of international life outside our borders. We were like a child in an adult world, privileged to enjoy the typical egocentricity of the child, if not his dependence on others. But today that egocentricity is no longer permissible. It has yielded to the responsibilities of maturity just as in individual life the irresponsibility of the child yields to the obligations of maturity and parenthood.

Today our own dependence on our foreign environment has grown to the dimension of a vital interest of our society. Yet we have to recognize that this foreign environment is in some measure what we make of it, that it is extensively influenced by the way we behave ourselves. And the most important thing to be realized is that this exertion of influence takes place, for better or for worse, whether we mean it to do so or not. It flows of itself from our relative physical weight in the world and from the growing crowdedness of the planet we inhabit. We have become, as I have had occasion to say before, like a giant in a crowded room: we may wish to have nothing to do with the others, but everywhere we move we crowd someone or step on someone, and we have no choice but to recognize the resulting social obligation.

I submit, therefore, that in defining in our own minds the objects to which we consider our society now to be dedicated, we take as our point of departure the condition to which our development has already brought us at this time; that we recognize that the advance of our society along the lines of its traditional ideals is no longer something that can be realized just within the framework of our national life itself, but that it must be pursued at least partly in the broader theater of our international environment; and that accordingly we make it our object so to conduct ourselves in our capacity as a member of the world community as to enhance the chances for the preservation of the values we cherish here at home.

This may not seem too different from what we have thought and done in the past, but to my mind there is an important distinction. What I am talking about means that we must be prepared to make real sacrifices and painful adjustments in our domestic life for the sake of the health of our world environment—not just those sacrifices in the form of military expenditures which we are accustomed to thinking of as a prerequisite to the assurance of our military security, but sacrifices in phases of our lives which we have never learned to think of in connection with foreign affairs at all, and ones which would be directed to the positive formation of our relationship to the outside world rather than to the negative enterprise of military preparedness.

Now many people who would agree with me in all that I have just said would be inclined to suppose that the problem was merely one of the creation and cultivation of suitable multilateral institutions for the ironing out of the frictions between our national life and that of other people. They have felt that what was required was only the establishment of new forums where we could deal with the outside world in a different way from what we have in the past.

I am bound to say that to my mind this is not the correct approach. New institutional facilities may some day be required; but if so, they will come last on the list of the important things to be done, and not first. What seems to me to be of first and vital importance is something that we Americans have to do for ourselves and by ourselves, and that is to render our country fit and eligible for the sort of adjustment our foreign relationships are going to have to go through.

I have often had occasion to take issue with the enthusiasts for world government. I must still do so from the immediate political standpoint. But I would suggest that they are right in one thing, and that is in their appreciation that this country will not solve the problems of its developing world relationships except on the basis of a readiness to go in for an extensive merging of its life with that of other peoples. The difference between us is mainly about the way we should move toward this goal. The partisans of world government would have us reach out and embrace the entire world community all at once, through the immediate establishment of a new series of political relationships. I would have us start by tackling first the problem of our relationship with the peoples nearest and closest to us, and then to begin not by frightening them half to death with offers of our immediate intimacy but by doing things to ourselves which would mean that the prospect of our intimacy would no longer be so frightening. The best way for us to move toward any form of unification is to try to make it so far as possible a living reality, or at least a living possibility, by unilateral actions affecting the nature of our own society, before the problems of a formal contractual relationship are dealt with.

You will see that what I am pleading for here is a recognition of the fact that if our society, which has always been predicated on the experience of growth and expansion, is to retain its vitality, there must continue to be an expansion of the actual sphere in which our national life proceeds. But there could be nothing more tragic and unfortunate than that we should try to bring about this expansion by any means involving violence to the needs and feelings of peoples elsewhere. It must come on a voluntary basis and as a response to the needs of others as well as of ourselves. And it must be an expansion not restricted only to material things but one embracing our outlook, our vision, and our inner experience as human beings. It is in this sense that I am speaking when I express the conviction that the development of our society will not be a healthy one unless it envisages and works toward the ultimate merging of its social and political identity with those of at least certain other nations, and particularly those closest to us by tradition, by outlook, and by the circumstances of their world position. On the other hand, I am not pleading for "union now." I do not think this country is today in any condition to unite with anyone. Sometimes I think it is scarcely in a condition to unite with itself. And what I am proposing is that we make it our aim to do things which would put us in a position to expand the scope of our national life when time and circumstance become ripe for us to do so. Some of these things pertain to our relations with others; others pertain directly to ourselves.

The first and most important step in this great task is, as I see it, to change ourselves from an exclusive to a receptive nation in psychology and in practice. If we are to adjust to the demands of a new world position, the first thing we have to learn to do is to take as well as to give. I mean this in every sense: the economic, the demographic, the cultural, and the intellectual. There is no salvation for America in a frame of mind that tries to shut out its world environment.

This means, in the first place, that we must learn to accept the goods and services of others. Economic protectionism is not only an anomaly, but it is a ridiculous and ignominious expedient for a nation of our economic vigor and stature. What was right and necessary for a struggling underdeveloped country can be a form of infantile escapism for a strong and ostensibly mature one. If we have any real faith in those principles of free economic competition to which we believe ourselves to be dedicated, we should not be afraid of our ability to compete today on free economic terms with any nation in the world.

The same thing applies to the movement of people. If we are ever going to adjust our economic relationships with the older industrial areas of Europe, I am persuaded that we will have to permit a greater liberality of personal movement as between our country and theirs. This applies both to temporary travel and to freedom of permanent migration. So far as temporary travel is concerned, I am not impressed with the suggestion, which seems to me to be implicit in the present administration of our immigration laws, that our national security is going to be shaken if the Dean of Canterbury or some liberal European scholar visits our shores, or if some American playwright attends a gala première in Brussels. Such timidity is not the mark of a strong society. I am also not impressed with the argument that by greater liberality with regard to immigration our old American virtues would be swamped under a flood of uncouth newcomers. It is too late for all that. Immigration has been going on apace in this country for over a hundred years. The old American virtues, such as they were, are already dependent for their survival on the degree to which they can commend themselves to great masses of people who had no share in their origin. If we wanted to go in for this sort of protectionism, we should have started a hundred years ago. Today, America is either a cosmopolitan nation—a great cross-section of general humanity, distinguished from other nations not by any peculiarity of blood or color but only by geography and tradition and spirit—or it is nothing at all.

What I have just said about goods and people goes a thousand-fold for the world of the mind and the spirit. In this respect we Americans stand today at a crossroad of the most profound significance. Our national myth relates—let us remember—to an America which has long since ceased to be the real and dominant one. It relates to a rural America, an unmechanical America, an America without motor cars and television sets, an America of the barefoot boy and the whitewashed board fence, the America of the Webster cartoon. It was a wonderful old America. I sometimes wonder whether those of us who knew it will ever really adjust to any other. I hope its memory and its inspiration will never die. But it is not the America of today; and if we cling timorously to its image as the ceiling of our cultural outlook we not only run the risk of a deep and neurotic division within ourselves as between the dream and the reality, but we run the risk of becoming essentially a provincial nation, an eddy in the current of world thought, unable to receive stimulus and inspiration from without and unable to impart it to others. Such a situation, I promise you, will never meet the needs of our future international relationships. In the intellectual sense as in the demographic sense, we are either a cosmopolitan nation, part of the world stream of thought and feeling, or we are nothing at all. Smaller nations, weaker nations, nations less exposed by the very proportion of their physical weight in the world, might be able to get away with exclusiveness and provincialism and an intellectual remoteness from the feelings and preoccupations of mankind generally. Americans cannot. It will never be forgiven us if we attempt to do it. If this is the path we go, we shall never succeed in projecting to our neighbors in this world, not even to the best of our friends and partners, those bridges that will have to be projected if the pounding, surging traffic of the future world is to be carried.

Thus the first dictate of progress toward a better world is, it seems to me, that America must become more receptive and more outgoing. The second is that it must take a tighter control of its own life and evolve a greater sense of purpose with regard to the shaping of its own development. I realize that these words carry very far, that they are at odds with the original concept of the objects of American society, with the original *laissez faire* theory that the individual is always capable of perceiving and pursuing his own self-interest and that the best interests of society at large will always flow from his continuing to do so. I still believe in the soundness of that theory in many respects. I believe in it particularly with respect to the freedom of our business life, and I do so after spending some years in intimate contemplation of a world where the principle of free enterprise has been wholly abandoned. In suggesting that the United States needs a greater sense of purpose in its domestic life I am not suggesting the welfare state or any brand of socialization of the means of production or distribution. But I am suggesting that in certain ways we are going to have to take the development of our national life more tightly in hand and to shape it more consciously and vigorously with an eye to the demands of the future.

One of the things that I have in mind is the manner in which we treat our natural environment here on this North American territory. I think we can no longer permit the economic advance of our country to take place so extensively at the cost of the devastation of its natural resources and its natural beauty. I think that we shall have to take stock in the most careful manner of what is still left to us out of the original fund of topsoil and mineral resources and water tables and forests and wild life with which God had endowed this territory, and to ask ourselves in all good conscience what we are likely to need of all these things in the future in the light of the numerical expansion of our population and the growing technological demands of each individual citizen. Having done this, I think we are then going to have to chart out realistic guidelines for national action which would assure that these future needs will be met, and that they will be met without increasing the present disharmony between man and nature. We will have to find some means to make these guidelines respected and understood by the myriads of state and local authorities and individual entrepreneurs whose collaboration will be essential to their observance.

In closest connection with this must stand the continuous and careful study of the development of our dependence on other countries for materials vital to the functioning of our economy, and a conscious attempt to shape our relationships with other economies in all these matters in such a way that they have some stability and some firm foundation of mutual understanding and do not lead in the future to all sorts of crises and tensions and tragedies. This means forward thinking, frank talking in our dealings with others, and a determination not to let private interests stand in the way of a far-seeing and prudent approach to the solution of our resources problem.

Beyond this, I think we have to contrive to give attention to something else which is very hard to describe and will be harder still to tackle as a practical problem, but which nevertheless has a lot to do with our future ability to meet the demands of our world position. I am referring here to the unhealthy development of social and community relationships in many parts of our country by virtue of precipitous and uncontrolled technological changes. I have in mind particularly the partial disintegration of many of our large urban communities, the general deterioration of social environment in the large portions of those communities, and the chaotic and often unsatisfactory manner in which new communities are being permitted to come into existence. I am talking here, if you will, about the need for municipal and regional planning in the light of the undeniable fact that the arrangement of the physical facilities for living and working unquestionably has a great deal to do with the inner health and happiness of the individual and with his ability to develop to the maximum his possibilities as a citizen and a human being. I am aware that there are experts on this subject who would deny that these conditions are really serious enough to warrant concentrated attention and recognition as a problem at the national level. But I can only voice a personal conviction that their significance for all of us is greater than we generally realize. And whether or not I am right in this judgment, I would like to say that the way things are proceeding at present produces on the surface of our national life a number of depressing and discreditable phenomena which are visible to the world at large and are genuinely important from the standpoint of our relationships with other peoples. Blighted areas, filthy streets, community demoralization, juvenile delinquency, chaotic traffic conditions, utter disregard for esthetic and recreational values in urban development, and an obviously unsatisfactory geographic distribution of various facilities for homelife and work and recreation and shopping and worship: these things may not mark all our urban communities in conspicuous degree; but they mark enough of them to put a definite imprint on the image of our life that is carried to the world around us, and this is an imprint that leads others to feel that we are not really the masters of our own fate, that our society is not really under control, that we are being helplessly carried along by forces we do not have the courage or the vitality to master.

The same impression is conveyed by the extent to which we have permitted the satisfying of the cultural and recreational and in part even educational demands of our population to be dominated by the mass media and, ultimately, by the advertisers. A foreigner easily gains the impression that we are wholly indifferent to the possibilities inherent in the way such matters are handled; that here, as elsewhere, we have resigned ourselves helplessly to the workings of our economic system; and that we are content to move wherever that system carries us, regardless of the effect on the esthetic taste, the intellectual health, and the emotional freshness of our people.

I cannot overemphasize how unfortunate such impressions are from the standpoint of our developing world relationships. We know from personal life that only he is capable of exercising leadership over others who is capable of some real degree of mastery over himself. Peoples of the world are not going to be inclined to accept leadership from a country which they feel is drifting in its own internal development and drifting into bad and dangerous waters. Even if we feel that we do not need this greater measure of control from the standpoint of the requirements of our own society, I suggest that we may nevertheless need it for the sake of the external impression if our own national life is to become a source of inspiration to peoples elsewhere.

To the extent that we are able to devise and implement programs of national action that look toward the creation of a genuinely healthy relationship both of man to nature and of man to himself, we will then, for the first time, have something to say to people elsewhere of an entirely different order than the things we have had to say to them hitherto. To the extent that we are able to develop a social purpose in our own society, our life and our experiences will become interesting and meaningful to peoples in other parts of the world. We must remember that we are practically the only country that has been able to afford for any length of time the luxury of this experimentation with the uninhibited flow of self-interest. Almost everywhere else, men are convinced that the answers to their problems are to be found in the acceptance of a high degree of collective responsibility and discipline. To many of them, the sight of an America in which there is visible no higher social goal than the self-enrichment of the individual, and where that self-enrichment takes place primarily in material goods and gadgets that are of doubtful utility in the achievement of the deeper satisfactions of life—this sight fails to inspire either confidence or enthusiasm. The world knows we can make automobiles and television sets and that we can distribute them, but it is looking to us for other things as well, things more relevant to the deeper needs of men everywhere. No matter what we may think, individually, of the TVA, it should give us all pause for thought that no other American undertaking has ever commanded more interest and respect in the world beyond our borders.

Now this problem of the adjustment of man to his natural resources, and the problem of how such things as industrialization and urbanization can be accepted without destroying the traditional values of a civilization and corrupting the inner vitality of its life—these things are not only the problems of America; they are the problems of men everywhere. To the extent that we Americans become able to show that we are aware of these problems, and that we are approaching them with coherent and effective ideas of our own which we have the courage to put into effect in our own lives, to that extent a new dimension will come into our relations with the peoples beyond our borders, to that extent, in fact, the dreams of these earlier generations of Americans who saw us as leaders and helpers to the peoples of the world at large will begin to take on flesh and reality.

There is one last point to be added. I have spoken here primarily of things that had to do with our physical environment. I would like to say that probably more important than any of these things, in the ultimate effect on our foreign relations, will be the things we do in this coming period with respect to our own inner American selves and the state of our national soul.

This is a hard and cruel world we live in. It contains many spectres, many horrors, many appalling situations. No one who travels widely or lives extensively beyond our borders can fail to feel at times a sinking of the heart at the depth and complexity of our world problems, at the degree of misery and hatred and bewilderment by which human life is attended in other parts of the world, at the envy and jealousy we face, at the hideousness and reality of the threats to our security. I have personally had to look at these things over some eighteen years of foreign residence, and many of them near the seat of the most calculated and intense political antagonism that any nation has ever faced, and I think I know what a *tour de force* it is going to be if this nation succeeds in conducting for long its rich and comfortable existence without real difficulty in a world of so much poverty and misery and frustration.

Yet if I were to ask myself what is the most frightening and menacing thing with which we are today confronted, I would say without hesitation that it is not something outside our society, but something within it. I am not thinking here only of that pathetic fringe of our population, now cowering three-fourths underground, that still finds solace for its ego in an association with the communist party. What I have in mind is far more serious than that. It is the much larger proportion of our people who find it impossible to accept the relatively minor and almost routine problem presented for us by the phenomenon of external penetration and subversion in our life without permitting it to become for them a source of loss of confidence in the integrity of our society as a whole. There can be nothing more disruptive of our success in every great area of foreign policy than the impression that we no longer believe in ourselves and that we are prepared to sacrifice the traditional values of our civilization to our fears rather than to defend those values with our faith. This is not just a question of the spectacle of a few men setting out to achieve a cheap political success by appealing to primitive reactions, by appealing to the uncertain, suspicious little savage that lies at the bottom of almost every human breast; it is more importantly the spectacle of millions of our citizens listening eagerly to these suggestions and then trotting off faithfully and anxiously, like the victims of some totalitarian brainwashing, to snoop and check up on their fellow citizens, to purge the libraries and the lecture platforms, to protect us all from the impact of ideas. The outside world knows perfectly well that no nation has ever had less need for this sort of thing than our own, that it responds to no real and commensurate requirement of our national situation, that it can only be the reflection of some deep inner crisis, some gnawing fear of ourselves.

If we wish to stride forward successfully in our relations with other peoples in this coming period, and this means in the development of our own civilization as a whole, then we must proceed with vigor and determination to conquer this demoralization, to recover our inner equilibrium, to teach ourselves again to act like what Americans really are, and not like what we fear they might be.

I am afraid I have taken you very far and very fast in these lectures. It is certainly a most imperfect picture I have presented to you. I have left many gaps. In many respects I am afraid I have raised more questions than I have answered.

But if there is any one impression I would hope I might have left in your minds, it is the impression of the essential unity of all the problems of our national behavior and accordingly of the unsoundness and danger implicit in any attempt to compartmentalize our thinking about the problems of foreign policy. We saw in the first of these lectures how our thought had been split by two separate planes of international reality. We subsequently looked more closely at each of these planes to determine the demands it placed on our national conduct. To my own mind, the upshot of these considerations is that it is in the inner development of our civilization—in what we are to ourselves and not what we are to others—that these two planes of international reality really come together. We will not find the unity of foreign policy for which we are concerned if we seek it only in the fashioning of relationships external to our national life. We will find it only in the recognition of the full solemnity of our obligation as Americans of the twentieth century: the

119

obligation of each of us, as an individual, to his God and his faith; the obligation of all of us, as a political society, to our own national ideals and through those ideals to the wider human community of which we are in ever increasing measure a part.